MEET HIM AT THE MANGER

MEET HIM
AT THE MANGER

STUART & JILL BRISCOE

Harold Shaw Publishers, Wheaton, Illinois

Unless otherwise indicated, all Scripture quotations are taken from *The Holy Bible: New International Version.* Copyright 1973, 1978, 1984 by the International Bible Society. Used by permission of Zondervan Publishing House. All rights reserved.

The Scripture quotations marked NRSV are from the New Revised Standard Version of the Bible, copyright 1989 by the Division of Christian Education of the National Council of the Churches of Christ in the United States of America, and are used by permission. All rights reserved.

The Scripture quotations marked KJV are from the *King James Version.*

ISBN 0-87788-557-5

Compiled by Vinita Hampton Wright
Edited by Robert Brown and Mary Horner Collins
Cover and interior design by David LaPlaca

Library of Congress Cataloging in Publication Data

Briscoe, D. Stuart.
    Meet Him at the manger : discovering the heart of Christmas / Stuart and Jill Briscoe.
      p. cm.
    ISBN 0-87788-557-5 (cloth)
      1. Christmas. 2. Jesus Christ—Nativity. I. Briscoe, Jill. II. Title.
    BV45.B694 1996
    263'.91—dc20   96-18174
                                               CIP

02 01 00 99 98 97 96

10 9 8 7 6 5 4 3 2 1

CONTENTS

Che First Christmas

CHRISCMAS NOW

ACKNOWLEDGMENTS

"Lion of Judah," "He Laid It Down," "A Royal Birth," "Afterwards," "Room In My Inn," and "Christmas Now" are reprinted from *Heartbeat* by Jill Briscoe, © 1991, Harold Shaw Publishers, Wheaton, Illinois 60189.

The poem "Choosing to Be Chosen" is reprinted with permission from *Wings* by Jill Briscoe, published by Victor Books (1988), SP Publications, Inc., Wheaton, IL 60187.

"Time, Not Things" first appeared in *Virtue* magazine, in Jill Briscoe's column "Full Circle."

"Behind Tinsel Trivialities" first appeared in *Virtue* magazine, Nov/Dec 1993, in Jill Briscoe's column "Full Circle."

THE HEART
OF CHRISTMAS

ADVENT: THE CHRIST CHILD COMES

There are certain signals we all recognize that warn us Christmas is on its way. The day after Thanksgiving, the busiest shopping day of the year, reminds us that Christmas is near. Holiday advertising is everywhere we look and in everything we hear. Christmas jingles won't let us forget what is just around the corner. We're told of every financing plan imaginable to ensure that we can afford all the gifts we "need" to buy for all the people on our growing list. Magazines assume their "Christmas look," and retailers put on their most elaborate displays. Families begin the task of tying all their loose ends together, in the hope that for at least a few days they can "be a family" in the holiday spirit.

The most significant indicator, however, that a special day is drawing near is on our church calendar: the beginning of Advent. The season of Advent is the time we prepare, not for extra expenditures of cash, but to remember the Christ child who came to live among us. We attempt, once again, to consider that God actually assumed our humanity and was born and entered our world in order to secure our redemption.

So while we will no doubt be caught up in all the hurried

activity of the Christmas season, let us also take time in this Advent season to prepare our hearts to welcome once again the God who laid aside his glory and assumed our humanity because of his great love for us. There are few truths in this world that can be more wonderful, more startling, more exciting than this.

WINTER WITHOUT CHRISTMAS

While walking around the shopping mall during the Christmas season one year, I was reminded of our trips to the Holy Land. These were whirlwind trips, and we would be exhausted by the end of each day. I recall asking an older gentleman, "Did you enjoy the tour today?" He replied, "Today I ran where Jesus walked!" And Christmas time at the mall can make you feel just like that. Running and rushing. It's hectic, it's noisy, it's tiring. Worst of all, most of the time it's winter without Christmas.

Despite the charming Christmas music and bright displays, winter sometimes prevails. While people race through this holiday period, disillusionment, anxiety, and depression often tighten their icy grip on human hearts. Many people don't realize that we can choose to have Christmas in the winter of our hearts, right now.

I remember years ago my mother traveling from her beautiful home in England's lake district to visit us in our tiny cottage. We were serving a youth center at that time, and we didn't have much money. Yet when my mother left, she quietly and wistfully said to me, "God lives here, doesn't he,

Jill?" I said, "Yes, Mom." And I went on to say, as gently as I could, "I'd rather live in my cottage with Jesus than in my castle without him." She and I both knew that I had lived in a beautiful manor house—like a castle. But we were both learning that a person is more than the things he or she possesses.

We are more than what we buy and possess. We are more than our celebrations. When we worry over the Christmas expenses and exhaust ourselves trying to keep everything up and running for all the family events, let us remember that this is merely winter. The cold winds of winter constantly whirl around us. But we can invite Christmas into our hearts during this and all other seasons.

Pause in the midst of the frantic holiday pace and praise God for Christmas. Make room for Christmas in winter.

GOD'S GRAND COMMUNICATION

Christmas is many things to many people: a celebration, a cosmic visit, a time for family traditions. I'd like for us to see it in one more way: Christmas is a communication. It is God saying something to human beings, something that they would have no clue about except that God decided to say it:

> Do not be afraid. I bring you good news of great joy that will be for all the people. Today in the town of David a Savior has been born to you; he is Christ the Lord. This will be a sign to you: You will find a baby wrapped in strips of cloth and lying in a manger. (Luke 2:10-12)

God is desperately concerned that we understand the truth about ourselves and about his interest in us. Centuries ago, in an ordinary world, in the midst of all kinds of bad news and at a time when most people had little reason to expect anything good, a baby was born. Through the great void of silence and despair, God shouted a message to us loud and clear.

It was a communication of joyful assurance: "Do not be afraid. I bring you good news of great joy." Why should the angels be singing above this small planet, so insignificant in a huge universe? What could possibly have happened to make the heavens over small Bethlehem split open to reveal a totally different dimension? There was joy in heaven; a host of beings knowing something we humans didn't yet know—a wonderful thing had taken place in our midst.

It was a communication of grand dimensions: "I bring you good news of great joy that will be for all the people." This good news and this joy incorporates all people everywhere. That straw-filled cubby hole in Bethlehem has become the doorway to the rest of the world, not only at this time but for all time.

It was a communication of glorious significance: "Today in the town of David a Savior has been born to you; he is Christ the Lord." There have been, and will be, many "saviors." Many great people have walked in this world, leading people to something better, helping them learn a little more truth, teaching them a better way to live. So the birth of a savior was not terribly significant. But this savior was also the Christ, the promised Messiah. This child was *the* Savior! This child was "Christ the Lord," which in Old Testament terms referred to God himself. God had come to visit the earth and all the people on it. This indeed was significant news.

The angel goes on to say a seemingly insignificant thing. "This will be a sign to you: You will find a baby wrapped in strips of cloth and lying in a manger." No doubt there was more than one baby lying wrapped up in strips of cloth at that time and in that place. For the poor of that day, who had nothing else to wrap a baby in, that was nothing unusual. But to put a baby in a manger was most unusual. And so, the sign is given to them. "You can go and hunt around Bethlehem, but you're only going to find one baby, a poor little baby, wrapped up in strips of cloth lying in a manger—that is the One." Scripture has always insisted that God's message be verifiable. You can check out what God says and find it to be true.

There are a lot of people who give an academic nod to the Christmas story. They would have absolutely no problem nodding their way through this statement, "Do not be afraid. I bring you good news of great joy that will be for all the people." Who wouldn't nod in agreement to a communication of this nature? But how many of us would actually go search for the baby, would dare to prove God true?

God has communicated Christmas to us so that we might verify it as true in our lives. He wants us to go, like the shepherds, and see if the Savior has really come. Has God actually visited you, where you live, in the middle of your ordinary life? Do you have the energy, the curiosity, or the will to come to the manger yourself and see what you find?

At Christmas time God cups his hands over his mouth, as it were, and shouts at the top of his voice, so that with all the din going on around them, human beings might hear what he has to say: "Listen! I've got great news that will bring you glorious joy!"

Meditate on the doorway of heaven flying open with joyous, thunderous praises of angels ringing out. Try to comprehend the grand dimensions of their message. Listen carefully to what God is communicating. He has something important to say to all of us, in all places and at all times, and it's a message worth listening to.

SPIRITUAL DAWNING

The people walking in darkness have seen a great light; on those living in the land of the shadow of death a light has dawned. (Isa. 9:2)

What does it mean to have something dawn on you? Does it mean your understanding is lit up as a new day is lit up with the dawn? Jesus has come to redeem us. Has it really dawned on you what that means? God intends for all of us to have a personal spiritual dawning.

I remember at the age of fourteen being in the Swiss Alps just after World War II. One day I decided to get up early to watch the dawn. (The first chapter of Romans tells us we can clearly see God in his creation.) I was full of bright ideas at that age, but I was not a believer at the time. I never went to church, didn't read my Bible, and wasn't thinking about Christian things. I just got up to see the dawn. And sitting in the Swiss Alps, I saw an incredible display of God's creative genius as the dawn came. I was so overcome, I ran back to my bedroom, grabbed a stub of a pencil, and scribbled my first bit of poetry. It wasn't very good poetry, but it went something like this:

The day dawned softly, filling me with awe.
It seemed the other side of heaven's door.

That God forgives my sin is plain today;
In spite of my sin, the sun did rise again.

It's amazing how God can speak to us in spite of our biblical ignorance. I think that morning was the first ray of light for me, the beginning of my spiritual dawn even though I wasn't really fully enlightened to the gospel until years later. Dawn dispels the darkness, and it began there for me.

Peter tells us, "We have the word of the prophets made more certain, and you will do well to pay attention to it, as to a light shining in a dark place, until the day dawns and the morning star rises in your hearts" (2 Pet. 1:19). Have you considered the fact that you need a personal spiritual dawn? That the morning star is meant to rise in your own heart? We all sit in darkness until we're enlightened by Jesus Christ, the light of the world. In Revelation 22:16, Jesus calls himself "the bright Morning Star."

Several years after my experience in the Swiss Alps, I was sick in the hospital. I was sitting in the middle of my own darkness. Jenny, one of my hospital mates, was very sick, but she had the Light of the World shining in her life. The Son of Righteousness had risen in her life with healing in his wings. Jenny's body was ill, but she was whole in her spirit.

With the Holy Spirit's help, Jenny removed my spiritual blindfold. She took me to the manger to see the brightness of the dawn. A sunbeam infant, visiting our dark humanity, lay in a manger. When I saw the heavenly dawn among the donkeys, my heart began to beat rapidly. I asked Jenny how I could possibly thank God for entering my personal darkness. She said, "Well, just ask him into your life. Thank him personally." And so I did. That was the moment a spiritual dawn exploded across my dark horizon.

Dawn in our Disobedience

I've often talked with people who argue against the Christian gospel on supposedly intellectual grounds. I don't do very well in those situations. I get impatient and tongue-tied. Sometimes people tie me up in knots. But I often say to them, *"Will* you believe, not *do* you believe?" Most of us have reasons for not believing. A part of us just doesn't want to be good. What we need to say is, "God, I really don't want to be good. Make me want to want to. Dawn in my heart. Forgive me for not wanting to be good." That's where it all begins.

Light transforms everything it touches. Take time to watch the sunrise some morning. Notice how radically the light changes absolutely everything it touches. The dawn of Christ is just like that. Even in all the dark corners of our disobedience, the rising of the Morning Star can transform us.

Dawn in our Disappointments

Zechariah needed dawn in the midst of disappointment. All his life he had prayed for a child. Now he and his wife, Elizabeth, were old. But in his old age he finally got the opportunity to enter the Holy of Holies and present the daily offering. In Zechariah's day, this was a once-in-a-lifetime opportunity. And as Zechariah carefully followed the prescribed temple rituals, an angel appeared to him, frightening him out

of his wits. The angel said, "Zechariah, I've come because of your prayer."

I can imagine Zechariah wondering, *Which prayer? The prayer about getting the Romans off our backs? About Israel turning back to God? About my rheumatism?* And the angel said, "No, not those prayers. *The* prayer . . . about the baby." And Zechariah probably thought, *Huh? Oh, that prayer.* I wonder when he had stopped praying that prayer—undoubtedly years before.

But you see, God never lets your prayers fall to the ground. Years after we've stopped praying, God answers our prayers. Sometimes we don't even recognize when God answers because we've forgotten all about it. But God in his grace answers anyway. So the baby came and the dawn rose on Zechariah's disappointments.

Are you like Zechariah? Have you been sitting in darkness because of a lifetime of disappointments? Zechariah wasn't what we would call a bad person; he was quite devout, probably a righteous man in human terms. Yet disappointment had set its shadow over his life. And then the light dawned.

Dawn in our Disability

Or maybe you're like Joni Eareckson Tada. Joni needed the dawn in her life. As hard as she tried, Joni couldn't get into the Christmas spirit one year. It was Christmas Eve and she was seated in the church with her friends. Candles lined the sanctuary. Boughs of green pine decked with red ribbon were everywhere. Soft snow swirled outside. Everything was perfect. Except inside Joni. There she sat in darkness.

Joni Eareckson Tada is paralyzed from the neck down. As

the congregation sang, she did not feel a single stirring of adoration or praise. *It's no use,* she thought. *I'm such a failure.* Then the bittersweet strains of a familiar carol reached her heart. "O come, O come Emmanuel, and ransom captive Israel that mourns in lonely exile here." This described her feelings exactly. "O come, Thou Dayspring, come and cheer our spirits by Thine advent here. Disperse the gloomy clouds of night, and death's dark shadows put to flight." In the depths of her soul, Joni cried out, "That's how I feel!" Then she bowed her head and asked the Lord to take away her gloom and bring her joy. And he did. There went the darkness of disability.

Whether it's disobedience, disappointment, disability, or whatever you want to use to fill in the blank, Jesus comes to dawn on every form of our darkness. Has the dawn come to your life, and yet you haven't recognized it? Are you looking for that first ray of light? Is your Christmas this year a bleak one? Concentrate on that first beam—the Christ child in the manger. Sit still with the God who sends the dawn, and watch all that this Christ-light will transform in your life.

DAWN IN MY DARKNESS

Dawn in my darkness, deep in my heart.
Tell all the shadows to swiftly depart.
Send out your love light,
Dispelling despair.
Dawn in my darkness,
Tell me you're there.

Dawn in the drabness of dreary days,
Color my life with perpetual praise.
Paint with your paintbrush
A heavenly view.
Dawn in my darkness,
Tell me it's you.

Dawn in my darkness, bring me new hope.
Wake up my spirit and help me to cope.
Use me to tell others
Just who you are.
My dayspring, my sunrise,
My bright morning star.

GOD SEEKING US

ou can go around the world and find a wide variety of religions. Yet all world religions tend to have one thing in common: People are seeking God. They seek God through any number of philosophical systems or cultural practices, trying to do whatever it takes to make a connection with God.

But Christianity is different: *God is seeking us.* This is what Christmas is really about; it is God pursuing humanity. The coming of the Christ child has nothing to do with people trying to unravel the mysteries of God through their own intellectual or mystical abilities. In that little child in the manger, *God* took the initiative and revealed himself to us. Let me illustrate what it means that God came looking for us through a story recorded in the book of Luke.

> Jesus entered Jericho and was passing through. A man was there by the name of Zacchaeus; he was a chief tax collector and was wealthy. He wanted to see who Jesus was, but being a short man he could not, because of the crowd. So he ran ahead and climbed a sycamore-fig tree to see him, since Jesus was coming that way.

When Jesus reached the spot, he looked up and said to him, "Zacchaeus, come down immediately. I must stay at your house today." So he came down at once and welcomed him gladly.

All the people saw this and began to mutter, "He has gone to be the guest of a 'sinner.' "

But Zacchaeus stood up and said to the Lord, "Look, Lord! Here and now I give half of my possessions to the poor, and if I have cheated anybody out of anything, I will pay back four times the amount."

Jesus said to him, "Today salvation has come to this house, because this man, too, is a son of Abraham. *For the Son of Man came to seek and to save what was lost."* (Luke 19:1-10, italics added)

Luke was rather interested in stories about tax collectors; there are no fewer than three in his gospel. Tax collectors in that cultural context were Jewish people who collaborated with the occupying Roman government to extract money from their own Jewish brothers and sisters. They were not usually well liked by the Jewish community.

Earlier in Luke we read about another tax collector, Levi, who was sitting at his tax booth. Jesus told him, "Follow me," and Levi left everything and followed Jesus. Later, Levi threw a big party, and the religious folk questioned Jesus' attendance—why would he eat with all those wicked cronies of Levi? Jesus said, "It is not the healthy who need a doctor, but the sick. *I have not come to call the righteous, but sinners to repentance"* (Luke 5:31-32, italics added).

These two stories tell us why Jesus came to us—to seek and save the lost, and to call sinners to repentance. Jesus actually delineates three categories with these statements: *the lost, the "righteous," and sinners.* Every human being fits into one of these categories. God came looking for each of us, regardless of where we fall in that spectrum.

God Seeks the Lost

I like the story of the young man in England who was driving through the countryside in his spiffy sports car. He screeched to a halt when he saw an old gentleman at a crossroads. The young man shouted at him, "I say, do you know how far it is to London?"

"No," the old gentleman said.

"Well, do you know which direction it is to London?"

"No."

"Can you tell me what time it is?"

"Can't say that I can, young man."

"I say, you don't know much, do you?"

"No, but I'm not lost."

We've all come across people who know an awful lot, but they are very lost. And many times, they don't know that they're lost. All of us have been in the "lost" category at some time. People are made for God, but they have lost God, and they may be driving around looking good and sounding intelligent, but they are totally disoriented. Sometimes they feel that life isn't making a lot of sense, but they don't know why. That's what we mean by lostness.

The word "lost" in Scripture is sometimes translated as "perish." To perish is to slowly deteriorate. Can't we relate to this? Sometimes we sit down and look at our lives in light of where we were ten years ago, and we're horrified to discover how far we've come. Yet we are hard put to see how we got to where we are. It's been a slow, insidious, careless, undisciplined deterioration of spirit. Sometimes we look at

habits that dominate us, and we remember when we thought we had so much control over our lives. That's lostness.

Wherever you look, people's lives seem to be unraveling. They make a wrong decision or take a wrong turn, and suddenly their lives are in shambles. There are many people who have started life's journey on the wrong premise, have based actions on wrong conclusions, and who will finish up at the wrong destination unless something changes dramatically. That's what we mean by lostness.

The good news is that God came looking for people who are lost and wandering and disoriented.

God seeks the self-righteous

"I have not come to call the righteous," Jesus said. But from everything else Jesus said about human nature, we know that he was using the term "righteous" tongue-in-cheek, for in fact no one is righteous in the sight of God. Jesus came to show the self-righteous what they were really made of, and he was quite straightforward when he talked to them about their spiritual condition.

His strongest words were for "righteous" people—those people who claimed to be members of God's covenant people; who, when it served their purposes, could recite Scripture by the hour. But when you scratched the surface of their spirituality, there was little difference between them and the people who were blatantly immoral. The only difference between the "righteous" and "sinners" was that the righteous shrouded their immorality under a cloak of religion.

Why did Jesus confront the religious "sinners"? Because

Jesus came seeking those who are self-deceived into thinking they are righteous.

God Seeks Sinners

In Luke 18, we meet another tax collector. Two men are praying to God, one a "righteous" Pharisee, the other a "sinner"—a tax collector. In New Testament language, a sinner was a person who was openly, blatantly immoral. A sinner was one who flatly ignored God's laws and didn't really care that he was doing so. Tax collectors were known as traitors and cheats because Rome turned a blind eye to any extra money these people collected for themselves. To the Jewish community, a tax collector was certainly a sinner.

But Jesus came looking for just such people as these. And today God is still looking for sinners of all varieties—those people we know who thumb their noses at authority and morality, those who sell out to the highest bidder, those who do as they like and don't care what others think of them.

Whether we are hardhearted sinners, self-deluded religious folk, or people who have become disoriented and whose spirits have deteriorated, in Christ, God comes looking for all of us. The baby Jesus was born into a world full of people who are lost, and the man Jesus seeks us out to bring us back to God. This is the essence of Christmas.

BEHIND TINSEL TRIVIALITIES

Somehow the pull is strong each year to rummage through boxes, silver paper, and tinsel trivialities, looking for Bethlehem. For the first eighteen years of my life, all I knew of Christmas was the party in the middle of hard winter. It seemed a good idea, a family reunion in our beautiful English home.

Even now, I can almost smell the chestnuts roasting in the blaze of the living room fireplace, and I can almost hear the soothing voice of Bing Crosby crooning my father's favorite: "I'm Dreaming of a White Christmas." I see the games we played, like the huge jigsaw puzzle around which the whole family would gather, squealing with triumph when each person successfully fitted a piece. I remember the faces of loving family members and friends, the guests who would come and go, bringing fruitcake and nuts, adding to the music each night around my father's electric organ.

That was as near as our family got to tipping a hat in God's direction: a wonderful winter celebration, usually happy and loud, but not *Christ*mas. Happy Hoopla, yes. Joyful Noel, no. How many lovely family parties, like ours, will be held in

Christendom this year, I wonder. How many times will I need to remind myself, amid the trappings of tree decorating and gift buying, of my conversion?

It was in college that I discovered what Christmas was really all about—how God became a baby for me! He came to earth at Christmas because he knew I needed eternal life; the Christ child was the only way to the Father. I reeled in horror at the realization of how our family's benign neglect must have offended Jesus! We had been throwing a big bash for him for years, but never invited him along. I knelt, then lay flat, face down in my little college bedroom, crying: "Jesus, I'm sorry. I'm so sorry. Help me make good those eighteen years!"

At Christmas break, as I traveled by train back home to Liverpool, my mind raced ahead to December 25. This was to be my very first real Christmas. What would I do that I had never done? What wouldn't I do that had become tradition? I didn't know. So I went through various scenarios, practicing my lines: "Mother, let's ask Jesus to his party this year." No, that would be too much. "Father, let's sing carols instead of 'Rudolph.'" No, they wouldn't want to do that.

At home, my struggle intensified. I scanned the newspaper for a local church with a Christmas Eve midnight service. The one I found was miles away, and I knew I would need to walk home. Public transport would be halted for the holiday by that hour. I decided it didn't matter; I was going.

I slipped away on Christmas Eve as family and friends were happily singing around the organ, "sleigh bells jingling, ting, ting, tingling. . . ." I found the little chapel crammed with people. Candles lit faces that reflected eyes full of wonder, love, and praise. Jesus was here! We sang at the top of our lungs, hearts bursting with thanksgiving for Divinity in the shape of a man-child, bringing us back from the dead. We prayed and smiled knowingly at one another, total strangers bound by a belief that brought us together to worship the Christ child. It was a bit of heaven on earth. I didn't want it to end. But it did.

The walk home took two hours, down deserted streets, past homes lighted with holiday glow, amid the scent of roasting chestnuts, and the chiming laughter of family togetherness. This was like the scene waiting for me at my parents' home. I slowed my steps, wanting to sing all the carols I knew at the top of my lungs one more time, telling my world what God had done. But I was home.

On the doorstep, I could hear the party inside revving up. I slipped into the pack as unobtrusively as I could, but my mother's friend saw me.

"Why, here she is," she said louder than I'd wished. "We didn't know where you were!"

"She's been to church," my sister interjected.

"How do you know?" asked her friend.

My sister smiled softly. "Look at her face."

Eyes turned to me. There was a sudden quietness. I went pink. What were they looking at? My cheeks were surely stinging from the cold, but there seemed to be something more catching this bunch's attention.

Apparently they saw Him. I was content. Partying without praising was for the birds. They knew I was changed. Another day I would explain why. Now it was time to slip up to Mom, Dad, and my beloved sister, give them a kiss and wish them from the bottom of my heart a Christmas without winter.

THE REASON FOR THE SEASON

"**I**n the beginning was the Word, and the Word was with God, and the Word was God. He was in the beginning with God. . . . And the Word became flesh and lived among us, and we have seen his glory, the glory as of a father's only son, full of grace and truth" (John 1:1-2, 14, NRSV). This passage of Scripture may not seem related to Christmas at first. But it tells us something incredible. The eternal God who was before all things determined to leave eternity, break into time, take upon himself our humanity, and be born as a baby. Can it really be true that the invisible God, the idea behind all things, the moving force who existed before all things, came to earth as a baby of Bethlehem? I believe so. But why?

GOD SPEAKING OUR LANGUAGE

It's impossible for us to comprehend God. Just as you can't

pour an ocean into a thimble, so you can't fit the mind of God into the human brain. So God decided that he would translate himself into a language humans could understand. And that was why Jesus was born. He came to interpret God to us in our own language. The invisible God doesn't make sense to us without Jesus, the visible expression of God. "In the beginning was the Word, and the Word was with God, and the Word was God." And the Word became a baby in order to interpret God to us.

The Word became flesh in order to identify with us. How does God identify with a mere mortal? Let's look at the facts of Jesus' birth and early life.

"He was born of a virgin" (Luke 1:34). His mother was pregnant before she should have been—not a big issue these days, but certainly a big issue in that culture and time. That meant that Jesus was ostracized by many people from the beginning, because his very birth was questionable in the community.

"There was no room for them at the inn" (Luke 2:7). Jesus' parents had no place to stay, and thus he was born in a stable. Jesus was homeless right from the very beginning of his life.

"Take the child and escape to Egypt" (Matt. 2:13-14). Soon after Jesus' birth, the paranoid and murderous king Herod forced Mary and Joseph to flee for their lives to Egypt. Jesus and his family were refugees for two years.

Jesus could easily have chosen to be born in very different circumstances, but he came to identify with ordinary people. Ordinary people live in stressful circumstances. Ordinary people are surrounded by misunderstanding about who they are and what they are about. In Jesus, God identified with humanity at every point of our pain.

God, whom we can't see and don't know, is interpreted to us in Christ. He didn't sit in heaven indifferent to our pain, but identified with us in Christ, even to the point of taking upon himself our sin. Out of love, the sinless One chose to die a shameful death on a cross. He dealt with the one thing that stood between us and God.

So as we travel to that long-ago manger to meet the Christ child, let us see more clearly the Father who sent him. A child in a manger is not intimidating. A child is meek and gentle. But the child can lead us to the man who is Jesus. This is the reason for the season.

A CHRISTMAS PRAYER

Dear Lord,

At this busy Advent season, may we take time to be still and be nourished in our spirits. May Christ be born and live powerfully in our lives, and may it be evident to all that the Holy Spirit has given birth to something powerful, attractive, compelling, and true in us. Amen.

the divine design

the visit

There are so many ways to celebrate Christmas. It's different in America than in England, my home. And those of German, Korean, Italian, or other heritage would agree that Americans celebrate Christmas in a very different way from their own countries.

When I first came to live in America, we experienced our first American Christmas soon after arriving. A number of traditions and terms seemed strange to us and the children. For instance, "Father Christmas" became "Santa Claus." But it was fun seeing Christmas celebrated in a different way.

All these years later, I'm not always sure which terms are English and which are American. But one word I do remember well is *visit*. Now, in England, a visit doesn't mean that you just drop by for a while some afternoon. It means to come and stay—most surely overnight and probably several successive overnights.

A couple of weeks after moving here, Stuart said to me, "There are eight or ten people coming to visit." I took a whole day making up that many beds. I thought, *How am I going to provide sleeping quarters for all these people? And I won-*

der how long they're coming for? In England, a visit can last anywhere from a week to three weeks or more. When Stuart came home, he asked, "What are these beds doing all over the place?" I said, "Well, you said all these people were coming to visit."

Sometimes I prefer the King James Version of the Bible because the words simply hold more meaning for me. I love the way the song of Zechariah reads in Luke 1:76-79:

> And thou, child, shalt be called the prophet of the Highest: for thou shalt go before the face of the Lord to prepare his ways; To give knowledge of salvation unto his people by the remission of their sins, Through the tender mercy of our God; whereby the dayspring from on high hath visited us, To give light to them that sit in darkness and in the shadow of death, to guide our feet into the way of peace.

The dayspring has come to visit us, and this is certainly the English sense of the word. (I knew God was an Englishman all the time!) He came the first time to earth to stay a long overnight—thirty-three years of visiting. Jesus did not just drop in; he came with the purpose of staying in the guest room of our lives. We often put him in the back, in the "stable" so to speak. But he didn't come for that reason. He came to stay, to settle in. But why has he come? What has he come to do on this visit?

The Greek word for *visit* which is used in the Scripture passage above means something like a doctor who is coming to visit a sick patient. Somebody decides that this person is so sick the doctor must move in to take care of the person. The doctor is saying, "I need to visit this person, to observe her, to reflect on this illness, to find a cure." The dayspring on high, Jesus the dawn of heaven, came to our world to stay overnight, to settle in, to look at this sin-sick person called the human race. He came for a long-term visit in order to assess the damage, diagnose the problem, and establish a cure.

We have been visited by the dawn from heaven, not just for a brief time, but long enough to make a difference. And Jesus came not that we might be host to him, but to settle in and take care of us. Jesus brought some of his "home" with him, which is heaven in our hearts now, and in the eternity to come.

the waiting is over

half the fun of Christmas is waiting for its arrival. Children, and many adults, can hardly stand the tantalizing anticipation of fun and gifts. But even apart from Christmas, a lot of people spend their lives waiting. They wait for the perfect love or the perfect job or the perfect home or the perfect situation. Some people are waiting for something that will never appear—because it doesn't exist. This is one of life's absurdities, waiting for something we're not sure of or something that is unrealistic to hope for. In this sense, waiting is a tragic waste of time. But some people are waiting for more than unrealistic dreams. Their hopes have foundation. And the assurance of their hopes gives them the strength to carry on, sometimes in very difficult circumstances.

A history of anticipation

The nation of Israel had a long tradition of waiting. We see

in the Old Testament that at least a few people in every generation had set their hopes on what God would do. Abraham had been living in rather comfortable circumstances when the Lord appeared to him and told him to leave his home and occupation and go somewhere—a place God would show Abraham when he got there! It's incredible that Abraham was prepared to uproot his family on such inadequate information! But eventually he arrived in the land of the Canaanites, and God made a threefold covenant with Abraham.

God promised that everywhere Abraham placed his feet would become his land. God promised Abraham that a very large nation would descend from him. (This was an incredible thing for Abraham to believe. You remember that he was rather elderly, childless, and without any prospects of having children.) Lastly, God told him that this great nation would be a means of blessing for all the nations of the earth.

But after Abraham's children had been born and he had begun to see these promises come to pass, he died. And the nation he had started came under bondage to the Egyptians. For many years the Israelites waited for their circumstances to change and for God's promises to be fulfilled. When God called Moses and led the people out of bondage, he brought them to Mt. Horeb and confirmed once again the covenant he had made with Abraham.

Moses died without entering the Promised Land. Joshua led the people into the land. Their wait for a homeland was over! Unfortunately, once they got into the land, they forgot the Lord. They began to worship other gods. Morally and spiritually, they began to fall into decline. Politically and economically, they ran into great problems. And it was only a matter of time until they were taken away into captivity by the Assyrians and then the Babylonians. Things went from bad to worse.

Eventually the people in bondage were released and returned to their land. They tried to rebuild their broken-down capital, Jerusalem. They put up another temple which was a poor representation of the glory that had once symbolized their nation. They worked at getting back their culture, religion, and their moral base, but nothing was really the same again. And a lot of people just hung around bemoaning the good old days, hopeless and helpless.

It was into these bleak circumstances that God raised up his prophets. One of the best known prophets was a man called Isaiah. Isaiah, along with all of God's other prophets, was to remember the great covenant God had made with their ancestor Abraham. God had punished his people for their disobedience to that covenant. But God, in his great mercy and forgiveness, gave his prophets a message of comfort and consolation for his discouraged people:

> Comfort, comfort my people, says your God. Speak tenderly to Jerusalem, and proclaim to her that her hard service has been completed, that her sin has been paid for, that she has received from the LORD's hand double for all her sins. (Isa. 40:1-2)

The phrase *speak tenderly* means literally "speak to their hearts." In other words, "Sense their need, their deepest longing; empathize with them at the point of their deepest deprivation. Tell them that I can address them in the depths of their hearts' needs." What a wonderful message this was that Isaiah and his contemporaries were given to pass on to God's people! They had gone through hard times as a direct consequence of their rebellion against God. But now their sin was being dealt with. The punishment for sin had been concluded. There was now no condemnation for them. And the day was coming when this message would come loud and clear to their hearts, and they would be comforted.

More Waiting

Centuries later, in the New Testament, we find the tradition of waiting continued. In Luke 2, which tells us the story of Jesus' birth and the events that immediately followed, we find the story of two people who were waiting. One was Simeon, who was waiting for the "consolation of Israel." The other person was Anna. She was looking forward to the "redemption of Jerusalem." They saw the baby Jesus as the answer to their waiting, and they both rejoiced.

Others waited too. Joseph of Arimathea, a highly respected man, was the man who, after Christ's crucifixion, requested to take down Jesus' body to give it a decent burial. We're told that Joseph was waiting for "the kingdom."

After the resurrection of Christ, two of his disciples were walking along the road to Emmaus. Unaware of Jesus' resurrection, they were disconsolate. And someone—the risen Christ, whom they did not recognize—drew alongside and began to speak with them. When Jesus asked them why they were looking so sad, they said, "We had hoped that [Jesus] was the one who would redeem Israel."

Under Roman domination, Israel had fallen on very hard times. At that time, probably every member of the harassed Jewish nation was clinging to some sort of hope, waiting desperately for deliverance. But some people, like Simeon, Anna, Joseph, and the disciples heading toward Emmaus, were waiting with focused hope. They were staking everything on the prophecies in the Old Testament that redemption would come. They honestly believed that at the moment of Israel's greatest need, God had raised up Isaiah and other prophets in the past and given them a message of comfort and consolation. They, like their parents, grandparents, and great-grandparents, were eagerly waiting for God to burst into their circumstances and do what he had promised to do.

Light for All

How tragic it is that often people live in despair, believing that what they *have* is all there is to being a person. And yet what tremendous consolation to realize that there is much more to life than our present trouble. Those Israelites who paid any attention to their heritage knew that there was more. Their people had hoped in a God who brought something more to life's experience. But many people outside Israel's borders had no such hope. They didn't have the prophecies, the promise of blessing.

When Simeon looked upon the baby Jesus in the temple, he said an incredible thing:

> My eyes have seen your salvation, which you have prepared in the presence of all peoples, a light for revelation to the Gentiles and for glory to your people Israel. (Luke 2:30-32, NRSV)

This child was the hope not only for the Jews, but for all other people as well. Were the Gentiles in such bad shape? Well, this is what some of the Gentile philosophers were saying at about that time: "Best of all for mortals is to never have been born. But for those who have been born, to die as soon as possible is best." Many sages regarded life as punishment and birth as humanity's greatest misfortune. The

world was evil. Life on earth brought sorrow. This earthly body was a prison of the spirit. Even if there is no hope of a hereafter, the grave would be a welcome place of rest.

This dark outlook is still with us today. Allow me to paraphrase Bertrand Russell, the brilliant philosopher who lived in England not long ago:

> Man is the product of causes which have no pre-vision of the end they are achieving. His origins, his growth, his hopes and fears, his loves and his beliefs are but the outcome of accidental collation of atoms. No fire, no heroism, no intensity of thought and feeling can preserve an individual life beyond the grave.

The Gentiles certainly needed some light to banish their hopeless despair. And we today need something promising to wait for. What we need is the consolation of Israel! We are *not* an accident. Our experience cannot be reduced to randomly colliding atoms. Life has a grand design and a grand Designer. There is hope.

Some people spend their lives waiting. But they don't know what they are waiting for; they only know that there must be more to life. Others have had a picture of the hope for centuries, and they are waiting too. The great news is that the object of our anticipation has come to us. Christmas commemorates the end of a long, long wait.

GOD BECAME FLESH

I'm sure you've sometimes grumbled about the way the world news is covered. I know I have. I get very frustrated when I realize the whole of the news is going to be covered in half an hour. That's why I'm glad we have a few programs, at least, that try to look at situations with a little more depth.

Yet these "sound bytes" of information seem to satisfy a good many people. Rather than really thinking through the issues of the day, people want someone else to do their thinking for them. They want information packaged in capsule form to make the few catchy slogans go down easily. This is all some people want to bother with. Tragically, such a passive approach leads to a very superficial understanding of the world in which we live.

There's no shortage of half-hearted greetings and superficial slogans about Christmas either. I don't know how many people have wished me "happy holidays" or have hoped that I have a "blessed and merry Christmas." Many others have said to me, "The compliments of the season to you." All this is good and appropriate. But we are in real danger of reducing Christmas to superficial sound bytes, and un-

fortunately, many of the sad people around us are satisfied with a slogan or two.

Yet the substance of Christmas can be summed up in one incredibly brief statement: "The Word became flesh and made his dwelling among us. We have seen his glory" (John 1:14). If this were our greeting, instead of "Happy holidays," perhaps the season celebrations would have more depth to them.

God Living Among Us

I'm absolutely convinced that our understanding of Christianity stands or falls on what we believe about this statement "the Word became flesh." I would ask you a very serious question this Christmas season: Do you really believe the Word—God—became flesh?

I understand why people don't believe that "the Word became flesh." After all, it's a ridiculous statement, unless it's true. And if it's true, then the almighty God, Creator of the universe, has been in our midst. That's a discomforting thought. Think of it: God—the Word—became a person and lived among us persons. It does seem to be a logically incompatible statement. If he's God, he's God; if he's man, he's man. But he certainly can't be both at once. However, this logic assumes that we know everything there is to know about both God and human beings. And, if we don't know everything about them, how can we possibly conclude that God becoming a person is impossible?

Today many people who don't believe that the Word became flesh still celebrate Christmas. All of us want the festivities and the good feelings of the season. There's no question that the light that comes from God through Christ shines on all people. But that does not mean that all people automatically live in the good of it. The sun shines on everybody, but you can live in a cave if you wish.

However, this fundamental truth requires more from us. If God has become a person, this presents a problem. Scripture says that in Christ we have seen the God of the universe. He has already been here. It's one thing to think of an adorable baby surrounded by gentle beasts; but are we ready to deal with the reality of God living among us, revealing himself to us?

Seeing jesus' Glory

If we jump ahead and consider God living among us as the man Jesus of Nazareth, we see Jesus dying on a cross *for our sakes*. At that time, crucifixions were ordinary, everyday occurrences—nothing special. And it was not unusual for a good person to die on a Roman cross. Undoubtedly many innocent people suffered such torture at the hands of the oppressive Roman government. No, Jesus' dying on a cross was not a wonderful thing for us—unless he was indeed the Word made flesh. If he was God come to us in order to settle something permanently, then the cross and the resurrection were both events that demand our attention and our response.

What makes sense of the crucifixion is the incarnation. Incomprehensibly, God became a person, became flesh. It is God in Christ, God as man, and nobody else, dying on the cross, assuming our sin, who has something to offer to our world. The book of John says, "We saw his glory." The apostles and others saw the glory of God in a person, who lived among them and spoke to them. They saw Jesus glorified in

his death and resurrection. We too can see his glory. All this is possible because on Christmas day, the eternal Word became flesh.

In the Christmas manger we must see the wonder and marvel of the Word made flesh. Jesus' glory remains veiled to us if we don't, and thus we trivialize Christmas. If we see his true glory, then we will worship him truly.

WHAT JESUS SAID ABOUT HIS COMING

The heart of Christmas is the fact that God sent his Son, Jesus, to be born in a manger. But why? Many Bible commentators have unraveled some of the mysteries of the Old Testament prophetic passages about Jesus' life and worked out their theologies. But let's look at some statements Jesus himself said about why he came.

"I have come in my Father's name." (John 5:43)

This means, literally, that Jesus came to represent his Father. In fact, another paraphrase of this verse reads: "I have come to you representing my Father" *(The Living Bible)*. The Lord Jesus came into this world with the express intention of making the invisible God visible, to make the unknown God known. He came into this world to make the unreachable God reachable. Seeing Jesus and seeing the Father were one in the same.

It's easy for us to rely on our own perceptions of God, because then we can make God into the kind of god we want. In the end, however, the God we face will be the God Jesus

came to show us. He came and interpreted a mysterious being into our kind of being. And if that was all he had come to do, that would be amazing enough.

> *"Do not think that I have come to abolish the Law or the Prophets; I have not come to abolish them but to fulfill them." (Matt. 5:17)*

God gave the law—the Ten Commandments—to Moses and the people of Israel for several reasons. One reason that I want us to focus on is the law as a representation of God. This was a somewhat limited expression of who God was, but it set God apart from all the false gods in the cultures around the Hebrew people. The law expressed to God's people the kind of life he wanted them to live. It set up protections for them and gave them healthy, holy standards. Unfortunately, God was giving human beings instructions that they could not, ultimately, fulfill. And our failure to carry out the law condemns us.

It's interesting to listen to people talk about how they "live by the Ten Commandments." Either they don't know what the Ten Commandments are or they are kidding themselves. The laws of God express a standard of living that fallen human beings simply cannot fulfill on their own.

Now, we might have wanted Jesus to come and just do away with this impossible law. "Give us a break, Lord!" But Jesus came and lived out the law in front of us; he fulfilled the law. Not only that, but he also amplified the law. If you think the Ten Commandments are tough, take a close look at the Sermon on the Mount in Matthew 5–7.

The law tells us not to commit adultery; Jesus tells us that even lustful thinking is a sin against God. So when Jesus came, he refocused our attention away from the letter of the law toward the essence of the law. And then he fulfilled it.

In fulfilling the law, Jesus showed us how we are to live.

No one would know what human beings are supposed to really be like if Jesus hadn't come. We wouldn't have a clue. We look at theories of human nature and behavior and say, "That's nice, in theory." But when we look at the life of Jesus, we say, "That's it!"

> *"I have come into the world as a light, so that no one who believes in me should stay in darkness." (John 12:46)*

Jesus came to bring not only spiritual illumination, but also intellectual, moral, and emotional illumination. I believe the Lord became a man to enter the many dark corners of human life and beam his light into the darkness.

The awful truth is that when the Lord Jesus came into the world as light, a lot of people turned him off for the very simple reason that they liked the darkness rather than the light. If you love darkness, you've got to turn the light off. And that's what has happened.

Have you ever talked with people who don't know God, or who have only a fuzzy or vague notion of him? Have you ever talked to some highly intelligent person who doesn't know God? This is one of the most frustrating things you can do! They're so smart, and yet, when it comes to knowing God, they're in the dark. The Lord Jesus came to invade the dark ignorance of even the sharpest mind.

We must always remember that people don't have light because for some reason they prefer the darkness. Sit down and contrast the two for them sometime. Some people have not thought through why they prefer darkness. Furthermore, they have come to fear the light or to think the light is something else. Jesus came to illuminate their understanding.

"The thief comes only to steal and kill and destroy. I came that they may have life, and have it abundantly."
(John 10:10, NRSV)

One basic rule of Bible study is to take a statement within its context. In the context of this passage, Jesus has been talking about a thief who sneaks into a sheepfold. A thief's triple objective is to steal, to kill, and to destroy. Jesus is saying, "I've come to do just the opposite. I don't take life, I give it."

Think of life in Christ in terms of what life is not. Anything that kills a person is opposed to all the life that Jesus came to give. Anything that robs a person of what he is intended to be as a human being is diametrically opposed to the life that Jesus Christ came to bring us. Christ came into the world to move into people's deadness and actually make that deadness of spirit come alive.

Isn't it thrilling to see Christ restore to people the areas of their lives that were dead, destroyed, and total losses? He came to transform our losses, to rebuild what has been torn down, to renew what is old and tired and full of despair.

"For this reason . . . I came into the world, to testify to the truth. Everyone on the side of truth listens to me."
(John 18:37)

This statement is part of the exchange between Pilate and Jesus before his execution, and is one of the most powerful confrontations ever recorded. Throughout the centuries, many have allied themselves with Pilate's answer: "What is truth?" The sole creed for some churches is the search for truth. Countless people spend their lives digging around in philosophies because they are searching for truth.

If we question everything then we get ourselves into philosophical knots, and we end up with nothing but the hollow question, *What is truth?* But at the core, we *know* that some things are simply true. They're right at some fundamental level. We know this to be so. Consider music, for example. You don't have to be a musician to know something is off pitch. Your ear just picks it up. Or think about architecture. We use a plumb line to ensure that the building is "true." If even one wall isn't true, according to that plumb line, the whole building is in trouble.

We know that some things must be true. At least we live as though some things must be true. Jesus is the source of all truth. He is the truth that makes a musical chord in tune and a plumb line plumb. Pilate unwittingly met truth in the very One he questioned. For all truth is God's truth, and Jesus is truth incarnate.

But at the sound of Jesus' true chord, my discord is uncovered. As the Lord Jesus lowers his plumb line, he reveals my crookedness. In the light of God's truth, my manipulation of the truth becomes known. This is what Jesus came to do. He came to represent the Father, to fulfill the law, to give light, to make life abundant, and to show us the truth. He said so himself.

he laid it down

hen it came time for us to emigrate to the United States, my husband said, "Sell everything! It's easier for the church leaders to provide a home for us over there." It seemed straightforward enough, just sell everything. But it wasn't so easy. Some things, yes—but not *everything!* What about the wedding presents, the sentimental keepsakes, the children's toys and dolls? We each had two cases: one for clothes, the other for personal things. I found, to my horror, my fingers firmly gripping much of what I thought I had surrendered to the Lord.

"Release my fingers, Lord," I prayed. He helped me to let go then, as he has helped me ever since. Several Christmases ago I wrote about letting go. First I read again Philippians 2:5-11:

> Your attitude should be the same as that of Christ Jesus:
> Who, being in very nature God, did not consider equality with God something to be grasped,
> but made himself nothing, taking the very nature of a servant, being made in human likeness.

And being found in appearance as a man, he
    humbled himself and became obedient to
    death—even death on a cross!
Therefore God exalted him to the highest place and
    gave him the name that is above every name,
that at the name of Jesus every knee should bow, in
    heaven and on earth and under the earth,
and every tongue confess that Jesus Christ is Lord, to
    the glory of God the Father.

After thinking about my clutching fingers, I wrote:

He came not trailing clouds of glory.
He came not wearing heaven's crown.
He left behind His father's golden city
And chose as birthplace Bethlehem's little town.

Equality with God was His by nature,
And worship by the angels was His right.
The honor due Him by His heavenly Father
He left to come and save us Christmas night.

He laid it down, He laid it down,
And taking human form became a man.
He laid it down, He laid it down,
And chose instead the world's redemptive plan.

So who am I to seek the world's dim glory?
And who am I to fight for worldly crown?
What right have I to choose to work in city,
In rural country or in tinsel town?

And who am I to grasp some vain ambition?
Or who to choose a partner for my days?

Am I superior to the Christ who saved me?
Do I have rights to keep or give away?

I'll lay them down, I'll lay them down,
And make Him Lord of all I want to be.
I'll lay them down, I'll lay them down,
Lay hold instead of all He wants for me!

CHRISCMAS is
SIMPLY DIVINE

There was a song on the radio the other day that told me all about the wonderful aspects of the Christmas season. Christmas is decorated trees and family feasts, fresh snow, children, and presents. Fortunately, Christmas goes beyond all that. Christmas is, simply, divine.

I know there are those who say that Christianity simply co-opted a pagan feast day in choosing to celebrate Christ's birth on December 25, thus perpetuating that pagan feast. I'm not saying there is anything special about December 25. But the original Christmas (on whatever day it occurred) was something special. It was, in fact, a divine event, in several ways.

> The people who walked in darkness have seen a great light; those who lived in a land of deep darkness—on them light has shined.
>
> You have multiplied the nation, you have increased its joy; they rejoice before you as with joy at the harvest, . . .
>
> For a child has been born for us, a son given to us; authority rests upon his shoulders; and he is named

Wonderful Counselor, Mighty God, Everlasting Father, Prince of Peace.

His authority shall grow continually, and there shall be endless peace for the throne of David and his kingdom. He will establish and uphold it with justice and with righteousness from this time onward and forevermore.

The zeal of the LORD of hosts will do this.
(Isa. 9:2-7, NRSV)

I love that phrase right at the end of this prophetic statement, "The zeal of the LORD of hosts will do this." Here Isaiah, moved by the Spirit of God, makes a prophetic statement which in all probability he himself didn't fully understand. God was taking the initiative.

Christmas: the divine initiative

If God had not taken the initiative to redeem fallen humanity by sending his Son into the world, there would have been no incarnation, no Christ, no Gospel, no reconciliation with him. If God had not acted, there would be no resurrection, no working of the Holy Spirit in our lives, and no revelation of God instructing us how to live. I'm so grateful that God took the initiative.

By saying, "The zeal of the LORD of hosts will do this," God is essentially saying, "I am the God of unshakable plans. I will accomplish everything I intend to accomplish, and nobody—nobody—will frustrate my plans." At Christmas time we must remind ourselves that *everything God had in mind for that original Christmas will come to pass.* The zeal of the Lord of hosts will accomplish it. This hope gives birth to confidence, and encouragement floods the human soul. God will do exactly what he said he would. We now have solid ground to walk on, and courage to live in righteousness, for the sovereign Lord of the universe will accomplish his purpose.

The title *Lord of hosts* means, "I am Commander in Chief of heaven's innumerable angels and unbelievable resources." The Lord of hosts stands, not only as a God of unshakable plans, but of unlimited resources as well. When he speaks, he speaks with ultimate authority. This was the initiative behind Christmas. *Christ came into the world with all the resources of heaven behind him.* All the forces of heaven stood on tiptoe, weapons in hand, anxiously awaiting his slightest command. Our view of Christmas must be seen as a divine initiative by a God of unlimited resources.

The word *zeal* means "enthusiasm." There's an awful lack of enthusiasm for the things that really matter. Some people seem to think that whatever we do, we must not become enthusiastic about religion. By all means, don't become too excited about Christ. Yet where we are concerned, God the Father is out-of-this-world enthusiastic about his children! And his enthusiasm inevitably becomes reality.

I think a lot of those who were part of that first Christmas weren't all that enthusiastic. Joseph certainly wasn't. Mary had her reservations. The innkeeper most definitely wasn't. And the people of Bethlehem couldn't have cared less. Maybe even some of the shepherds had reservations. But the one overriding factor—the zeal of the Lord of hosts—had every intent of going right on with the plan.

We need to remind ourselves that Christmas comes from divine initiative, the unshakable plans of a loving God with unlimited resources and unbounded enthusiasm. I sometimes like to think of God hopping all around heaven, full

of enthusiasm for the incarnation of his Son. That's true Christmas joy.

Do you find yourself caught up in his enthusiasm? Excited by his unshakable plans? Swept along by the mind-boggling concept of unlimited resources being released into your world? "The zeal of the LORD of hosts will do this." We can confidently write this next to every one of the promises of God.

Christmas: the Divine Invasion

A lot of people get upset about the Virgin Birth. But you can't evade the Virgin Birth when honestly studying the Scriptures. If you reject the Virgin Birth, you reject the clear teaching of God's Word.

I don't understand why people get so perturbed at the miraculous nature of Jesus' birth. If the zeal of the Lord of hosts will accomplish it, then nothing is impossible. The virgin Mary giving birth to Jesus by the power of the Holy Spirit is nothing less than the divine invasion of God into this world. This is a source of great joy. The fact that God brought his Son into the world in this way once again demonstrates his unlimited power and wisdom.

But if you think the Virgin Birth itself was a miracle, how about the eternal Son of God, the Second Person of the Trinity, coming to earth as a human being? Perhaps the great miracle is not so much a baby born of a virgin, but the awesome identity of the baby. This babe born of Mary was the one who created and still sustains the universe, holds all authority and power in heaven and on earth, and is the ultimate source of meaning and purpose for all creation. The Son of God vacated his heavenly throne for a stinking stable. This miraculous birth was nothing less than a divine invasion, where the Almighty Word of God became a fragile human baby, unable to speak.

But we have allowed the divine invasion of that initial Christmas to degenerate into something sentimental. We have lots of clean straw and colored lights and beautiful oxen and well-behaved donkeys. A lovely girl with a halo around her head sits among handsome shepherds kneeling, and regal wise men adoring. There they gather, beautifully and sentimentally around the manger in which the most magnificent child you ever did see slumbers silently.

Yet the Son of God was born to demonstrate his power and dominion: "For unto us a child is born, unto us a son is given; and the government shall be upon his shoulder. . . . Of the increase of his government and peace there shall be no end" (KJV). There was something majestic and eternal about this invasion. God came to earth as a human being in order to secure the redemption of his creation. What a divine idea!

PRINCE OF PEACE

The human heart always has and always will crave for peace. Ever since the Old Testament prophets predicted the coming of Messiah, God's people have cried out for peace. Invader followed invader, tragedy followed tragedy, awful holocaust followed awful holocaust in the long bloody history of the Jewish people. All the while, the prophets kept saying, "Better days await us." And they would always point to a coming era of great peace.

But many people have questioned this peace promised to Israel. Is there going to be a literal peace in a literal Israel in the Middle East? Can we look for this at some glad and glorious date in the future? Some look at the gathering of the forces in the Middle East and see it as a sign that Christ will come again and establish his kingdom reign. Other people say that the prophets meant that we should anticipate a spiritual peace in eternity, not a natural peace on earth.

We should be careful about our predictions of peace. Somebody is going to be wrong, and it could be all of us! There's always the possibility that God will come up with something none of us considered. What we do know is that at some

point Christ will reign at last, and that reign will be peaceful and eternal.

But the Bible also teaches that we can experience this eternal reign of peace now, *in our hearts,* as Jesus, the Prince of Peace, the God of Might, the Counselor of Wonders becomes the Lord of our lives. It is our experience of him in these ways that brings light into our darkness.

Where the Sovereign Lord rules over our relationships, they too can experience this peace. If we stop operating according to what the world tells us to be—economically driven, entertainment saturated, and ethically unrestrained— then his light can begin to shine into our darkness.

Most of us, at some time in our lives, have experienced real peace. But peace cannot be absolute or lasting without the Prince of Peace reigning in our lives. Let the Christ of Christmas bring peace to your life situation this holiday season.

the sharp edge of christmas

ost of us have received hundreds of Christmas cards in our lifetime, carrying a variety of beautiful messages. But imagine receiving a Christmas card that highlighted Jesus' statement, "I did not come to bring peace, but a sword" (Matt. 10:34). That would get your attention. How could the Prince of Peace say this? If we're to do justice to what the Lord taught about his incarnation, we must explore this shocking statement of Jesus.

Christ came to bring life, but some prefer death to life. Christ came to reveal the truth, but some reject the truth, accepting blindness instead. Christ came to call sinners to repentance, but some refuse to repent, choosing instead to live unforgiven. Christ came to seek and save the lost, but some turn away, remaining lost and disoriented. So we see that the good news of Christ's coming opens the way for great division between people.

Rarely do we think of the Christ child snuggled in the hay as a controversial figure. Yet King Herod considered him controversial enough to have all the infant boys around Jesus' age killed. Even while he was small Jesus brought a sword to the land.

And when Jesus' ministry began, there was plenty of controversy. He told his disciples to heal the sick, raise the dead, cleanse those who had leprosy, and drive out demons. The very arena in which his disciples operated was characterized by sickness, sorrow, social ostracism, and tension. Jesus dealt with a lot of evil spirits and a lot of suffering people. He constantly battled the sin and evil around him, including Satan himself. This is not a very peaceful picture.

Jesus' disciples took an aggressive position against these evils. When you confront sin and evil in its various social and personal forms, you wield a sword. Spiritual warfare is not conducive to peace, at least not initially.

Unfortunately, many people who profess the name of Christ do not see themselves as living in such an arena. Many in the contemporary church rejoice in the comfort zone of their salvation, rather than taking up spiritual arms to challenge and change the world. Yet Jesus gave his disciples authority to confront the society in which they lived.

The Bible says that the present age is evil. But the heavenly age to come will be characterized by righteousness, justice, peace, and grace. All evil, including sickness and disease, grief and sorrow, will be banished in the age to come. There will be no crying, no sorrow, only joy.

At the beginning of his ministry, Jesus announced that this very kingdom of heaven (or the age to come) was arriving, and was actually in their midst. The kingdom of God had arrived in the person of Jesus. Into this present evil age Jesus introduced the age to come. He taught his disciples that the kingdom was among them, and at the same to pray "thy kingdom come."

And today, as disciples of Christ, we are ambassadors of the coming kingdom. We speak on behalf of the King. And our lifestyle should convey something of the goodness, justice, and righteousness of the age that is on its way. This is what we are called to do.

Do we make a difference? Are we battling the evils around us? Christian churches should not be benign groups of people sitting in hermetically sealed communities, merely rejoicing in their own salvation, caring for their own, and entertaining their own. We are bringing in the kingdom. The Christ we follow was rejected, scourged, and crucified. If we truly confront this present evil age, we too may experience pain and suffering—the "sword."

Today, in many parts of the world, Christians do face the reality of this suffering daily. They realize that faithfully following Jesus may land them in prison, away from their families, for months and years on end. Many today lay down their lives for the sake of Christ. They demonstrate by their very lives the truth of Jesus' words, "I did not come to bring peace, but a sword."

A child was born into an evil world on that Christmas long ago. When he became a man, he took on the evil and offered new life to the world. Such a radical transformation will never be a peaceful process.

Lion of Judah

ion of Judah, great I AM,
   yet Son of God, gentle Lamb;
The One who made all human life,
   yet babe in womb of Joseph's wife.
Majestic One who naked came
   to dress Himself in human shame.
Naked twice—in crib, on cross,
   Lord of all who suffered loss.
Lion of Judah, great I AM,
   yet Son of God and gentle Lamb.

Lion of Judah, great I AM,
   yet Son of God, and gentle Lamb;
powerful voice of God Most High,
   limited to a baby's cry.
Mighty Father from above
   needing now a mother's love.
Helper, hope of Israel,
   helpless now Immanuel.

Lion of Judah, great I AM,
   yet Son of God and gentle Lamb.

Lion of Judah, great I AM,
   yet Son of God and gentle Lamb.
Majesty displayed in space
   lets me look into His face.
Meekness brings you near today,
   a Christmas babe in trough of hay.
A Mighty God, a tiny child,
   omnipotence so meek and mild.
Lion of Judah, great I AM,
   yet Son of God and gentle Lamb.

Lion of Judah, great I AM,
   yet Son of God and gentle Lamb.
You came to Joseph, shepherd, king,
   to those who needed songs to sing;
So hurting women, broken men,
   could find new life—be born again;
Because of Him, the gentle Lamb,
   Lion of Judah, great I AM!

A CHRISTMAS PRAYER

Dear God,

I've been searching for answers. I believe you sent your Son into the world to bring glorious gifts of liberty, joy, and meaning to people like me. It's hard to imagine such grace on my behalf, but you are a God of unbounded resources and unshakable plans. And so, Lord Jesus, I ask you to come into my life and establish your throne. I'm excited about the possibilities, because there is no end to your power and love. Thank you for what's going to happen. Amen.

THE FIRST
CHRISTMAS

A ROYAL BIRTH

Royal Birth,
God in embryo, growing to birth size
   a baby boy became.
Wrapped in swaddling bands of grace,
A light was lit in a bale of hay,
   setting the world on fire!

They called Him the carpenter's child.
They say he was brought up on Joseph's knees,
   playing with a piece of wood.
He went around healing people and
   being kind to sinners.
Christ His name . . .

God in Galilean robes
   dressed for battle . . .
Met the devil—paid the price—
and won the war!
Royal birth!
Royal life!
Royal death!
Royal resurrection!

joseph: a family problem

his is how the birth of Jesus Christ came about. His mother Mary was pledged to be married to Joseph, but before they came together, she was found to be with child through the Holy Spirit. Because Joseph her husband was a righteous man and did not want to expose her to public disgrace, he had in mind to divorce her quietly" (Matt. 1:18-19).

When I think of Joseph, I envision a young man tossing and turning in bed, trying to figure out what to do. Joseph had a big family problem. If you had asked him what he was thinking and how he was feeling, he might have said, "I have the heaviest heart, and I don't know what to think." He was, in fact, thinking of divorcing his wife.

Now Joseph and Mary were married. In the culture of the day, the marriage was done; the ceremony was over. All that remained was the consummation of it. In everyone's eyes, Mary was Joseph's wife. But she had just told him that she was pregnant. And since everyone knew that the consummation had not taken place (it, too, required a ceremony), Joseph was in great turmoil. His only solution was to divorce Mary as quietly as possible.

Joseph's story is pretty relevant to us, isn't it? You might be thinking, *That's me—I'm thinking about divorce this Christmas.* Maybe you're thinking about a divorce that's already happened or is about to happen or that seems likely down the road. Such thoughts remind us of close relationships now shattered and lying all in pieces. You've got a heavy heart.

The fact that Christmas is a *family* time makes it worse, doesn't it? When a family with broken relationships gathers to celebrate, it can be really difficult. A lot of people dread Christmas for that very reason.

During any Christmas season, there are families in trouble. Some years ago, while I was having a casual conversation with a college student, I happened to ask, "Are you going home for Christmas?" She said, "No, I'm going to be with friends. My folks want me to come home, but they've divorced since I was there last. And I don't want to go home and meet the woman who's taken my mother's place in my father's bed." A lot of people have heavy hearts, and they're tossing and turning as the holidays approach. Maybe you're living next door to a Joseph. Maybe you work with one.

> But after he had considered this, an angel of the Lord appeared to him in a dream and said, "Joseph son of David, do not be afraid to take Mary home as your wife, because what is conceived in her is from the Holy Spirit. She will give birth to a son, and you are to give him the name Jesus, because he will save his people from their sins. (Matt. 1:20-21)

God said to Joseph, "Take Mary as your wife. Don't be afraid to commit yourself to this marriage." Sometimes, of course, it may already be too late for a marriage. But perhaps God is talking to us, giving us a new plan of action, one that we need to consider seriously. When Mary told Joseph that she was pregnant, it was a bolt out of the blue. It didn't fit into any of Joseph's plans for their life together. And it was unlike any situation he had ever encountered.

But Joseph wanted to do the right thing. And, difficult as it was, he did what God told him to do. He took this pregnant girl to be his wife and set out on an adventure that the two of them would share. They would have to trust God through all the uncertainty and the questions from people who knew them. Joseph did an incredible thing: He welcomed the Christ child before the child was even born. While Christ was being formed within Mary, Joseph made a secure place for the incarnate Son of God to grow up in this world. He welcomed Jesus into an intact, stable family, not a wealthy or prestigious family, but a family under God's care and guidance.

Likewise, as we welcome the Christ child into the shambles of our everyday existence, God will help us as we go. Joseph was a believing man, and even believing people can have messy relationships. But the Christ child waits to be welcomed in, where he can grow in our lives and change us into God's true children.

MARY: THE ULTIMATE TRUST

he Holy Spirit will come upon you, and the power of the Most High will overshadow you. So the holy one to be born will be called the Son of God" (Luke 1:35).

Mary, the mother of Jesus, had a unique experience. She is the most celebrated woman of all time. Yet I believe that, in some significant ways, her experience parallels that of many women today. Maybe we can gain some encouragement from her story.

We begin with a young girl, probably no older than fourteen or fifteen. She lives in Nazareth, a small village of no more than 2,000 inhabitants. She is engaged to be married to Joseph. In Jewish culture, she was married to Joseph in all but the physical sense; to break this engagement meant taking a course of action as serious as divorce. Mary is a virgin. Joseph knows this; she knows this. (There have been many attempts to get around the fact that Mary was, literally, a virgin, but if we study the specific words that are used in the gospel accounts, we can't escape it.)

One day, an angel comes to Mary with the most incredible announcement: "Do not be afraid, Mary, you have found favor with God. You will be with child and give birth to a son, . . ." She would become pregnant by the Holy Spirit. Not only that, but the child conceived in her would be none other than the Son of God, who would be born in order that he might establish an eternal kingdom. Now that's quite a mind-blowing bit of information for a humble fourteen-year-old girl living in a little country town like Nazareth!

It's understandable that Mary should ask, "How can this possibly happen, since I'm a virgin?" She is told that this would be a work of the Holy Spirit. And the young girl says, in effect, "All right. I'm the Lord's servant. I'm open to what God wants to do with me. May all that you have said be fulfilled in my life."

Later, Mary visits her cousin Elizabeth, and Elizabeth says to her, "Blessed is she who has believed that what the Lord has said to her will be accomplished!" And Mary bursts into song, praising God: "My soul praises the Lord and my spirit rejoices in God my Savior" (Luke 1:45-47). How many people do you know who count it all joy and regard as a matter of praise the opportunity to make themselves utterly available to God? This is what Mary does. Even in a strange situation, facing a future with awesome possibilities, she is full of praise. She trusts that these things will actually work out in her life, and that this is reason enough for praise. She trusts the One to whom she is committed. That's the essence of faith.

Mary had good reason *not* to praise. She faced the embarrassing situation of a pregnancy that would obviously come earlier than anyone in her community expected. She had to explain all this to her immediate family and close friends. And she had no idea how this might affect her relationship to Joseph. Yet she trusted the grace of God. She believed that whatever God's purposes were for her, they were good, and she keenly anticipated nothing less than his best in her life.

I'm sure that once the people of Nazareth heard all the stories going around about young Mary, and saw the obvious changes in her physique, they were skeptical about it all. But Mary's submission to God's will gave her peace in the midst of the chaos.

We are told later that in the midst of this hubbub, Mary quietly treasured up in her heart all that was happening. Young Mary learned how to meditate. She learned to be still, to listen, and to observe. She learned to dig past surface appearances and to root her mind in the deeper spiritual realities. She received from the Lord great and wonderful promises. She mulled over them, treasured them, and prayed about them. She wanted to make sure that she understood them fully. She took the time to live in light of them:

> His mercy extends to those who fear him,
>> from generation to generation.
> He has performed mighty deeds with his arm;
>> he has scattered those who are proud in their
>> inmost thoughts.
> He has brought down rulers from their thrones
>> but has lifted up the humble.
> He has filled the hungry with good things
>> but has sent the rich away empty.
> He has helped his servant Israel,
>> remembering to be merciful
> to Abraham and his descendants forever,
>> even as he said to our fathers. (Luke 1:50-55)

Mary's praise, through eyes of faith, gave her insight into God's redemptive work in the wider world of proud rulers and humble servants, of rich and poor, and of Abraham and his descendants forever. When we trust God, who holds all futures in his hands, he sometimes gives us a glimpse into

his divine purposes on earth—a vision that would otherwise remain hidden from our eyes. This girl in her early teens already had a broader mind and clearer perspective than most people gain in an entire lifetime. God entrusted the Christ child to the care of this humble peasant girl who submitted her life to God.

Mary's humble submission to God marks out for us a challenging pattern to follow. She gave up all claims to her own body, her own reputation, her own future. With such faith, God will do great things, for nothing is impossible for him. At this Christmas season and throughout our lives, may we, like Mary, say to our Lord, "I am your servant. May your will be done in my life."

AFTERWARDS

O *bedience* is doing without the angel,
    doing the right thing by faith,
    because you know it's right.
Doing it without the feelings—
Luke says, "Then the angel left her . . ."
BUT JESUS HAD COME TO STAY!
Wasn't his name "IMMANUEL"?
I could imagine Mary wondering
    why the angel disappeared.

"Where was the angel when I had to face
    dear Joseph and tell him
    I had met the God of Grace?
Oh, where was the angel when he wouldn't
    listen to me and he called me
    a liar to my face?
And where was the angel who had promised
    me protection . . . yet let Caesar call
    a census in the land?

"And where was the angel when I needed
  my sweet mother,
  and nothing would work out as we had planned?
And where was the angel when we stood
  before the rest house
  and the keeper told us every room was taken?
And why were the angels talking to the shepherds
  when I was in the cave and felt forsaken?
Where was the angel when I cried aloud in childbirth,
  and the Son of God was born upon this earth?
Oh, where was the angel when Herod's murderous soldiers
  sought my baby boy upon his birth?

"Yet I didn't need to know the place of Gabriel's
  appointment,
  and I didn't need to hear the angels sing;
For marvelous though his person and wondrous
  though his comfort,
  'twas nothing to the presence of my King!
For *there* was the God of Grace when in the incarnation,
He visited my life and let me be
  a part of His plan—of His high and holy purpose
  as He lay within my arms and let me see—
A face sweeter than the angels,
  softer than the sunshine,
  and stronger than all the sons of light.

"Jesus Christ, my Savior, Immanuel, Redeemer,
The God of Glory, Majesty, and Might!"

the shepherds: least and lost

And there were shepherds living out in the fields nearby, keeping watch over their flocks at night. An angel of the Lord appeared to them, and the glory of the Lord shone around them, and they were terrified. (Luke 2:8-9)

Christmas proves that God takes a deep interest in the so-called "unimportant people." He arranged to have Jesus, the Son of God, born to a young peasant girl in an obscure village. It's almost as if God were going out of his way to say, "Listen, we know that people of privilege expect privilege. It's the underprivileged who never expect anything, so I'm going to aim at them. I'm going to give them the privilege of playing a leading role in my redemptive plan."

Take the shepherds, for example. In that cultural context, shepherds were nomadic lowlifes. When the gospel story tells us that there were shepherds living out in the fields, that's exactly what it means. They had to live by their wits in a rugged wilderness. They were rough folk who were always on the move, never putting down roots. When shepherds passed through town, people warned each other. Folks locked up their valuables and their daughters, keeping a respectable distance between townspeople and migrants.

These shepherds sleeping in the fields around Bethlehem were probably making an overnight stop on their way to Jerusalem. Shepherds had to drive their sheep from the plains,

where they had raised them, through the hill country to market in Jerusalem. (There was a law prohibiting sheepherding between Bethlehem and Jerusalem unless the sheep were bound for the temple; at that time the only place in Israel where breeding sheep was permitted was way out in the wilderness.) In Jerusalem the sheep would be sold and used for sacrifices in the temple. So the gypsy-like shepherds were leading their sheep to slaughter.

God sent a myriad of singing angels to announce the Good News to disliked and distrusted shepherds. In his unfathomable grace, God chose lowlife shepherds to be the first to hear of Christ's birth. Once again, the Lord of the universe demonstrated that he intentionally reaches out to the underprivileged, the dispossessed, the shunned, the lowly, and those without hope.

Humble people find it less difficult to accept the simple grace of God's Good News. The gospel runs counter to the world's ideas about self-worth and greatness. Christmas says we are sinners in need of a Savior. The humble are more likely to accept such uncomplimentary news. A sinful shepherd has nothing to lose in recognizing his need of grace; the proud must first overcome their pretentiousness and the pull of their possessions.

The humble can often take the gospel message where more high-profile people cannot. One of my favorite stories took place in Ethiopia. When missionaries first entered that country, they went to the royal palace and stated their intentions. One of the servants in the palace was commissioned to take these missionaries to one of the elite Ethiopian tribes. But without telling the missionaries, the servant chose instead to take them to his own dispossessed tribe. So the dispossessed group received the Christian message before the others. And God, with his wonderful sense of humor and his tremendous commitment to the underprivileged, used Christians from the lowly tribe to infiltrate the houses of the elite and wealthy with the message of the gospel. God works in strange and mysterious ways.

> The angel said to them, "Do not be afraid. I bring you good news of great joy that will be for all the people. Today in the town of David a Savior has been born to you; he is Christ the Lord. This will be a sign to you: You will find a baby wrapped in strips of cloth and lying in a manger."
> Suddenly a great company of the heavenly host appeared with the angel, praising God and saying, "Glory to God in the highest, and on earth peace to men on whom his favor rests."
> When the angels had left them and gone into heaven, the shepherds said to one another, "Let's go to Bethlehem and see this thing that has happened, which the Lord has told us about." (Luke 2:10-15)

Why a dramatic visit from angelic messengers? Because the people of Israel in those days had not heard a prophetic voice for hundreds of years. They were dull of hearing; their hearts were calloused. Their interest in the things of God was at a low ebb. With the angels' appearance God intervened into their affairs and burst onto the scene to grab their attention in no uncertain terms.

These least and lost shepherds listened to the angel's message, and in the midst of this encounter "the glory of the Lord shone around them." It is impossible for any human being in a natural condition to look upon God and survive. But occasionally, in various ways, the Lord gives mortals a glimpse of his brilliant glory, majesty, and purity. That is what happened here. Although the shepherds probably had been told over and over again that they were worthless, God in his glory shined upon them.

A BOY WAS HE

A boy was he
Yet very God of very God
A child, yet wiser than his years.
A boy was he
Yet very God of very God
The Lord's own Lamb appears.
A boy was he
Yet very God of very God
A carpenter's apprentice skilled.
A boy was he
Yet very God of very God
The Lamb His will fulfills.

Divinity breathing in air
  with a boy's lungs:
Eternity eating a meal
  with a boy's joy:
The Trinity coming to stay

in a boy's house,
in a boy's pain,
in a boy's world.

A boy was he
Yet very God of very God
A Son loved deeply by His own.
A boy was he
Yet very God of very God
The Lamb so far from home.

Divinity breathing in air
    with a boy's lungs:
Eternity eating a meal
    with a boy's joy:
The Trinity coming to stay
    in a boy's house,
    in a boy's pain,
    in a boy's world.

Eminence contained
Immanence experienced
Holiness explained in a boy!
Truth read clearly,
Love loved dearly,
God known nearly
    in a boy!

A boy was he
Yet very God of very God
A child, yet wiser than his years.
A boy was he
Yet very God of very God
The Lord's own Lamb is here!

The Wise Men: Jesus Seekers

Much legend and tradition surrounds the story of the wise men. We're told that there were three wise men, that they were kings, that they came from the Orient, and that they found Jesus in the manger. None of this is clear from the account in Scripture.

The biblical account in Matthew 2:1-12 doesn't tell us how many there were or that they were kings. They were "Magi," wise men, literally meaning astronomers, astrologers or philosophers. We've all heard the well-known carol "We Three Kings of Orient Are." They came from "the east," but nowhere does the Bible tell us that they came from the Orient, at least not what we think of the Orient. When the gospel account refers to the star rising in the east, it's probably a round about way of saying the star at its first rising. And contrary to our Christmas pageants, the Scriptures don't tell us that the wise men found Jesus when he was still in the manger. In all probability, they didn't see Jesus until he was a two-year-old.

So there are many elements of the wise men's story that have grown out of tradition and lack of information. But these

wise men who came from far away and laid their gifts at the feet of the infant Jesus, still have much to teach us. They were true Jesus seekers. But why would these men even embark on such a search? Based on what little we know about them, let's take a look at what may have motivated them.

A QUEST FOR TRUTH

These wise men were probably astrologers or astronomers—men highly respected for their wisdom. Astrology is based on the idea that the movement of the stars powerfully influences the affairs of humanity. Those who hold such beliefs spend a great deal of time trying to understand what stellar movements in the heavens might mean for life on earth. These men, possibly descendants of the soothsayers in Daniel's time (Daniel 2:2), studied the stars to discover truth. They wanted to know something of the hidden, inner workings of the universe.

However, beyond their curiosity, these men already had some knowledge of the truth. In part, that knowledge probably came through Jews who, in their historic captivities in Egypt, Assyria, and Babylon, had left many, many pieces of information concerning the Scriptures. And so these men not only had access to the insights of astronomy and philosophy, but to the vast riches of the Old Testament as well.

These magi, presumably from Babylon, went to considerable trouble to find this one to be born king of the Jews. What could possibly have motivated this interest? We know that magi advised kings in those days. And so the birth of a new king would at least have been of political interest to them. But they seem to be driven by more than politcal concerns. Something more significant was motivating their inquiry. And even though they engaged in astrology—which the Lord had specifically forbidden his people to be involved in—he still used their faulty understanding to lead them to the truth.

Contemporary American culture exhibits a great interest in spiritual matters of all sorts. But when you explore that spirituality, you find people all over the map. It is not traditional or historic spirituality, at least not the kind one would expect in a country with a Judeo-Christian heritage. We have many nominal Christians, inside and outside of the church, whose understanding of Christianity is mixed with all kinds of mysticism and New Age thinking—a synthesis of mutually contradictory teachings. But I believe God works in those with a spiritual hunger, even though they may be seeking spiritual truth where the truth cannot be found.

My wife gave a talk at a Christmas tea one year at a hotel in downtown Chicago. A lady came up to her afterward and said, "I'm a sorcerer, a magician. I have a business. I have never before heard the Christian's Christmas story, so someone invited me here today. And I'm so excited."

When Jill inquired why, she explained, "Last night I had a dream. Now I knew that Christians believed that Jesus was born in a manger, and Mary was the mother, but I have never, ever heard the details of the story, about Joseph and the angel visiting him, and all the other parts. As you began to read the whole story today from the Bible, my hair on the back of my neck stood up. I dreamed it last night, verse by verse, just as you read it!"

Jill was able to say that God had brought her there because there was a bigger "star"—pointing to Jesus—than the stars she had been involved with. This lady was a wise seeker, and she'll find the God whom she is seeking.

We must be able to communicate the gospel of Christ to the spiritually hungry, no matter what kind of spirituality

they're into. People wander winding paths of spirituality because they're really looking for the truth. They're looking for Christ, but they may not know that yet. The wise men were looking for some kind of king, but they certainly didn't understand the true nature and mission of the Christ child. Until we understand seekers, we won't be very effective in building bridges between them and Christ.

An intelligent Search

After the magi had gathered various clues about this Jewish king, they traveled to Jerusalem. Now if you're looking for the King of the Jews, what better place to start than Jerusalem, the capitol of the Jewish nation? Being wise men, they knew not to overlook the obvious. True wisdom doesn't make understanding complex, it makes the complex understandable.

People who profess to be seekers of truth commonly fail to approach their search intelligently. They are unwilling to look in the obvious places (such as the Bible and the Christian church, both of which have survived intact for centuries). And they are unwilling to work very hard. They want something to drop out of the sky into their laps. They're looking for an instantaneous experience that will change everything for them without any effort on their part.

That isn't the way it works. In the Sermon on the Mount, Jesus says, "Ask and it will be given to you; seek and you will find; knock and the door will be opened to you" (Matt. 7:7). To get a clearer sense of the force of the original, we could translate that verse, "Ask, and keep on asking . . . seek and keep on seeking . . . knock and keep on knocking." True seeking isn't a one-time shot; it takes time. It costs us immense emotional, mental, and spiritual energy.

A Diligent Search

When the magi got to Jerusalem, everything disintegrated. Imagine arriving at your destination after two long years of travel, only to have things fall apart. When the magi came to King Herod asking about the "one who has been born king of the Jews," Herod was scared and called together the wise men of Jerusalem to find out where the Messiah was to be born. He then secretly met with the magi with the pretense of sharing their concern for the search. He sent them to Bethlehem, saying, "As soon as you find him, report to me, so that I too may go and worship him" (Matt. 2:2, 8). But Herod had no such intentions. Herod was a paranoid, power-hungry murderer. He had no qualms about killing members of his own family. He really wanted to exterminate the possibility of this new king's arrival.

The wise men went to the right place and asked the right questions, but they were probably disappointed with the answer: "He's not here." And I imagine they might have been discouraged. But they didn't give up. They had come this far, and they weren't giving up now.

I wonder how easily you've been put off in your search. It's interesting to hear the reasons people give for ending their search. One person says they went to church, but because they couldn't understand the sermon, they didn't go back again. Or another person says they heard about someone's uncle who ran off with the church organist, and that's reason enough not to go to any church anywhere.

If we're serious about searching for God, we won't let anything get in our way. A genuine quest for God involves a lot of looking, reading, listening, and praying. If we're diligent in our search and ask honest questions, God will reveal himself to us, regardless of where we're coming from.

A RESPONSE OF WORSHIP

Many people start out seeking, but deep down they aren't willing to bow to anyone. So even if they find the Christ, their search will hold little satisfaction for them. Not so with the wise men. The wise men took their search to its logical conclusion. With wisdom and passion, they followed their clues and found the truth—the Christ child. And when they found Jesus, they fell at his feet and worshiped him. Their search may have begun out of sheer intellectual curiosity, but it ended in worship.

As part of their worship, the magi brought very valuable gifts to Jesus. Gold was a gift worthy of Christ's royalty. Frankincense was a gift to honor his deity. The bitter myrrh marked his humanity. Once they found who they were looking for, they didn't hold back.

Sometimes we search, but we're unwilling to open our lives to God once we find him. We withhold our love, our honesty, our past, our pride, our future. What was at stake for these wise men? Do you really think they expected to find the infant son of a peasant couple to be the King of the Jews? What might it mean to them politically to worship another human being, especially this human being in such unimpressive circumstances? What were they opening themselves up for, having acknowledged that this child held a position superior to theirs? Yet they set aside all these possibilities and gave their gifts.

Each of us in one way or another is searching and seeking. We must be wise in our seeking, seek wholeheartedly, and respond willingly and honestly to the truth we find. I pray that this Christmas season you will make room in your heart for seeking and worshiping the King.

ANNA: LOOKING FOR CONSOLATION

There was . . . a prophetess, Anna, the daughter of Phanuel, of the tribe of Asher. She was very old; she had lived with her husband seven years after her marriage, and then was a widow until she was eighty-four. She never left the temple but worshiped night and day, fasting and praying. Coming up to [Mary and Joseph], . . . she gave thanks to God and spoke about the child to all who were looking forward to the redemption of Jerusalem" (Luke 2:36-38).

Anna is a fascinating character. She was either eighty-four years old or well over a hundred. The Greek in this passage is a little ambiguous. It can mean that she was eighty-four or that she had been a widow for eighty-four years. Either way, she was a senior citizen. And she demonstrated four character qualities that should challenge us, whether we are eighty-four or twenty-four.

First of all, she was active. She was at least eighty-four and still serving the Lord every single day. Where did we ever get the attitude that "Well, I've done enough. Let the rest of them take over now. Time for a rest"? This idea certainly didn't originate in Scripture!

Second, Anna was alert. She was in touch with the Spirit enough to be in the right place at the right time. And she recognized the Messiah when Mary and Joseph brought him in for a seemingly routine ceremony.

Third, she was positive. It's unusual to see someone her age still looking *forward!* She wasn't looking back and talking about the good old days.

And, fourth, Anna was enthusiastic. The Scripture tells us that she approached Mary and Joseph giving thanks. We can imagine her saying, "Let me tell you something wonderful! I've just seen the child we've been waiting for these many years—the redemption of Israel!" She was no doubt stopping people, grabbing them by the arm, and showing them this baby. Maybe we should form an organization called "The Society of Anna" that would encourage us to be alert and enthusiastic throughout all our days on earth.

But there was more to Anna than enthusiasm. She wasn't merely a senior with a positive attitude; we need to understand the reality of Anna's circumstances. She was living in a place of utter desolation. Imagine being a widow for so many years in a land where there was no Social Security. Repeatedly, in both the Old and New Testaments, God gives instructions to Israel: Look after widows, because if you don't, nobody else will.

Yet, it doesn't appear that Anna felt sorry for herself. She didn't seem to be resisting the unfortunate situation of her life. The Scriptures say that she gave thanks and spent a lot of time worshiping, fasting, and praying. And when Joseph and Mary brought the baby Jesus into the temple to present him before the Lord, Anna recognized him for who he was. I think Anna could sense the wonder and the joy of Jesus' coming because her spirit was so sensitive to consolation. She had spent so many years alone. Now she knew that her Comforter had come.

There's a lot of desolation in our hearts today. "Comfort ye, comfort ye my people," says the Lord. There *is* a message of comfort and consolation in the One who has come to us, that child that dear Anna recognized on that day so many centuries ago. This child's coming has given us the potential to live a life of fullness despite our circumstances. The consolation of Israel has arrived, and in him there is hope.

A BETHLEHEM OF OUR OWN

uring this time of year I still become nostalgic for the English Christmases I once enjoyed. Many, many years ago I was a student at one of the colleges at Cambridge University in England. The campus is gorgeous. Miles and miles of oak-panelled corridors with well-worn flagstone floors connect the college's ancient and beautiful buildings. And every year, just before Christmas break, the Big Sisters knocked on the doors of the Little Sisters in the middle of the night. Soon a great procession of some four hundred or more girls, all dressed in white nightgowns and each carrying a candle, would begin to walk those old hallowed halls. For an hour or two, we wound our way up and down the corridors of that ancient campus, singing Christmas carols.

Needless to say, for a college full of women, most of whom never went to church, singing Christmas carols was difficult! Because of the religious traditions of England and of the college, most of us were familiar with the carols, but only the first few verses. Fortunately, someone had mimeographed the words of one carol, "Oh, Little Town of Bethlehem." And every so often the leader would begin this carol, and we all

felt secure singing it all the way through because we actually had the words to more than one verse.

I was caught up in the atmosphere of my surroundings, and in those moments I was overwhelmed with a sense of Jesus. My heart was opening up to the possibility of Jesus. And we came to verse three of the carol:

How silently, how silently,
*   the wondrous gift is given.*
So God imparts to human hearts,
*   the blessings of his heaven.*
No ear may hear his coming,
*   but in this world of sin,*
Where meek souls will receive him still,
*   the dear Christ enters in.*

I clutched my candle tightly, and I suppose I began to pray; although, since I'd never prayed, I wasn't sure how to go about it. But my soul was saying, *What do these words mean? How could it be? If only someone would tell me what it means.*

If you had stuck a microphone in the face of every single girl in that college just then and asked, "Do you think Jill's thoughts go anywhere beyond utter triviality?" they would have said, "No." And if you had asked, "Do you think she's got a hungry heart?" they would have laughed. Because at that time I was doing my own thing. I was involved with activities suited to a rebel. I had just been in a séance the night before, and I'd seen a Ouija board work. I wasn't really into those things, but I went right along with the crowd.

You see, I was like one of those shepherds. I'd always had low self-esteem and an incredible need to fit in and be accepted. I was also a bit like Mary and Joseph; I'd just broken an engagement.

But that night, God the Father walked down the staircase of heaven with a baby in his arms, and I began to understand. God began leading me to my Bethlehem. Actually, I arrived at Bethlehem sometime later, in a hospital room, but the words of that carol opened my soul to the reality of Christmas.

Have you been to Bethlehem yet? What do you believe about the Christ child? Will you come to a new understanding of Christmas this year?

A CHRISTMAS PRAYER

ear Lord,

For some of us the Christmas story is so familiar that it has become ho-hum. Please deliver us from this kind of response to your wonderful Good News. Let us see your glory in fresh ways. Open our hearts to the hallelujah chorus of the angelic hosts. Help us seek you as diligently as the wise men. Draw men and women, boys and girls to yourself this Christmas. May we all experience Christmas anew in our hearts. In Christ's name, Amen.

CHRISTMAS NOW

the spirit of christmas or the spirit of christ?

Once a year, toward the winter solstice, something odd happens. People start talking about peace and goodwill. They go out of their way to give, and they make efforts to forgive. Families that haven't got together, get together. A different atmosphere descends upon us—the spirit of Christmas.

There's a problem, however, with this annual spirit: It passes. We get very excited about the night before Christmas, but then we have to deal with the morning after Christmas. One woman described it to me this way, "It began to leave me last night," she said. "The old feelings started to come back." Most of us know what that means. The kindness, generosity, warm relationships, peace and goodwill we long for slip away when the "season" is over.

Many years ago, an older German man gave me one of the most striking illustrations of this quick passing of the season. He had fought with the German forces in the First World War—1914 to 1918. In those days they fought trench warfare. None of this high-tech stuff. Their combat was hand-to-hand. They dug trenches, and they fought in them and died

in them. These trenches were full of mud and blood and vermin. They were places of utter horror. The trenches were dug out in the fields of France so close to each other that enemies could actually hear each other talking.

This old gentleman told me that one cold, frosty Christmas Eve, they were huddled in the bottom of their trenches. There was no fighting going on, because the annual Christmas truce had been signed. Suddenly, from the British trenches a loud tenor voice, sweet and clear, began to sing "The Lord Is My Shepherd." And the sound floated up into the clear, moonlit air. And then, from the German trenches, a rich baritone voice tuned in, singing the same song in German. For a few moments everybody in both trenches concentrated on the sound of these two invisible singers, the harmony of the British soldier and the German soldier singing praise to the Lord who was their Shepherd. Then the singing stopped and the sound slowly died away. "We huddled in the bottom of our trenches," the old soldier said, "and tried to keep warm all night."

Then Christmas Day dawned. Early that morning some of the British soldiers climbed out of their trenches carrying a soccer ball. (The British take two things with them wherever they go— teapots and soccer balls!) They started kicking around the ball and had a pick-up game in no-man's land between the British and German trenches. Then, surprisingly, some of the German soldiers climbed out. And England played Germany in the no-man's land on Christmas Day in the middle of the battlefield in France during the First World War. England won! "Then we settled down and did the best we could for Christmas Day. The next morning the machine guns, bayonet fighting, and carnage resumed. Everything was back to normal."

That's how it is, isn't it? The spirit of Christmas will produce a truce, but it doesn't produce peace. The spirit of Christmas makes people think of peace and goodwill, but the strain of keeping it up is too great. The spirit of Christmas tells us a lot about the deepest longings of the human heart, but it also says something about the incapacities of the human heart. We need something more.

The spirit of Christmas needs to be superseded by the Spirit of Christ. The spirit of Christmas is annual; the Spirit of Christ is eternal. The spirit of Christmas is sentimental; the Spirit of Christ is supernatural. The spirit of Christmas is a human product; the Spirit of Christ is a divine person. That makes all the difference in the world. We read in the book of Luke about the difference the Holy Spirit made:

> In the sixth month, God sent the angel Gabriel to Nazareth, a town in Galilee, to a virgin pledged to be married to a man named Joseph, a descendant of David. The virgin's name was Mary. The angel went to her and said, "Greetings, you who are highly favored! The Lord is with you."
>
> Mary was greatly troubled at his words and wondered what kind of greeting this might be. But the angel said to her, "Do not be afraid, Mary, you have found favor with God. You will be with child and give birth to a son, and you are to give him the name Jesus. He will be great and will be called the Son of the Most High. The Lord God will give him the throne of his father David, and he will reign over the house of Jacob forever; his kingdom will never end."
>
> "How will this be," Mary asked the angel, "since I am a virgin?"
>
> The angel answered, "The Holy Spirit will come upon you, and the power of the Most High will overshadow you. So the holy one to be born will be called the Son of God. Even Elizabeth your relative is going to have a child in her old age, and she who was said to be barren is in her sixth month. For nothing is impossible with God."
>
> "I am the Lord's servant," Mary answered. "May it

be to me as you have said." Then the angel left her. (Luke 1:26-38)

The angel explained to Mary that she was actually going to experience the birth of Christ through the Holy Spirit in her life. The angel said to her that the power of the Almighty, through the Holy Spirit, was going to rest upon her. The baby to be born of Mary would be the One whose kingdom would never end. This light of Christ wouldn't flash into Mary's life and then die away. With the coming of this child, God was about to establish his eternal kingdom.

Christ can also be born in our lives. It is through the Holy Spirit that we are born again; it is a supernatural, spiritual work that makes us children of God, brought into his family and kingdom. The apostle Paul wrote to the Christians living in Galatia, "My dear children, for whom I am again in the pains of childbirth until Christ is formed in you" (Gal. 4:19). Paul was not talking about an annual event, but about a perpetual indwelling. The Spirit of Christ in us is not sentimental, beginning and ending with a sweet baby in a manger, but it is supernatural, powerful, and life-changing.

Living in the Spirit of Christ does not mean that people try hard to be more noble, good, and kind for a specific season every year. No. For Christians, God is in Christ reconciling the world to himself. The Holy Spirit enables people to be what they're not and to do what they can't. The Spirit of Christ is actually God, in Christ, through the Holy Spirit, being born in the lives of people, in all times and seasons.

Let us concentrate on experiencing the Spirit of Christ from December 25th right through next year—and the many years and Christmas seasons to come. The spirit of Christmas will come and go and be glamorized and trivialized. But all the while, the Spirit of Christ is being born into one person after another, and God's eternal kingdom is being established in our lives.

time, not things

ears ago as Christmas approached, our daughter and I sat down to figure out the family gift list. I don't know why it was usually left up to us to decide who gave what to whom, but that's how it was in our family. We came to the conclusion that none of us had everything we wanted, but all of us had everything we needed. The one thing we were all short on was time with each other. That year we decided to try an experiment and give each other time, not things. This necessitated some creative brainstorming and asking God for good ideas.

"Maybe the boys would enjoy tickets to the basketball game together," Judy suggested. "Perhaps you and I could go to a pretty Victorian tea shop and have English tea and a good talk together," I proposed.

Not all things we came up with cost money either. Judy gave her dad and herself a run in a charity race—something they had to train for and therefore spend precious moments with each other. One way or another that Christmas we managed to give each other the priceless gift of time.

After all, Jesus came that first Christmas night to give us

his time, thirty-three years of it, to be precise. What a gift! I'm so glad he didn't bring earthly gifts with him. Those are things that would only last a short time—treasures that moth and rust would undoubtedly corrupt, and where thieves could break in and steal.

This Christmas we may not have a lot of riches as the world sees it, but in giving ourselves to each other without reservation, as Jesus did when he came to earth, we can all know wealth beyond anything this poor world might have to offer!

ROOM IN MY INN

Room in my inn for my business affairs,
Room in my inn for my worries and cares,
Room in my inn for the drink and the smoke,
Room for the act, for the off-color joke,
Room for my family, room for my wife,
Room for my plans, Lord, but no room for Your life,
And room for depression, when the party's all through,
Room for myself, Lord, but no room for You!

Room in my stable, Lord, room out of sight,
Room in the darkness and room where it's night,
Room with the cattle, the pigs, and the sheep,
Room where a newborn babe can't get to sleep;
Room with the dirt, Lord, the rats and mice,
Room with the maggots and room with the lice.

Room, you can have it, how generous am I—
I like to be good when my Savior comes by;
Room in the filth and the mire of my sin,
Room on the Cross my redemption to win,
Room in my stable but no room in my inn!

the ox

When I was a little girl, my mother bought me an ABC book of Christmas. I still remember one verse, about the letter *O:*

> O is for Ox,
>   so gentle and mild
> Who gave up his stall
>   for the holy child.
> He didn't know why
>   the Savior had come,
> For no one had told him
>   of God and his Son.
> But then when he saw
>   all the light shining 'round,
> He knew it was Jesus
>   and knelt on the ground.

I really liked that verse when I was a little girl. Maybe that's when God's light first beamed into my life. I know how the ox feels. Whenever I see the cradle or manger at Christmas, even in a shopping mall, I just want to kneel

on the ground in worship like the old ox.

In Isaiah 1:3-4, the Lord says to his people, "The ox knows his master, the donkey his owner's manger, but Israel does not know, my people do not understand." The people who should have known all about God, didn't, and couldn't have cared less. In effect, God says, "My dog and cat pay more attention to me than you do." But when the ox "saw all the light shining 'round, he knew it was Jesus and knelt on the ground."

God's creation has no problem recognizing its Creator. But we do. We don't want to get rid of the darkness inside us. Jesus says, "This is the judgment, that the light has come into the world, and people loved darkness rather than light because their deeds were evil" (John 3:19, NRSV).

People don't want to come to the light because light has a way of revealing what's in the dark corners of our lives. A verse from a favorite Keswick hymnal of mine says,

> *Throw light into the darkened cells*
> *where passion reigns within;*
> *Quicken my conscience till it feels*
> *the loathsomeness of sin.*

CRIB, CROSS, AND CROWN

I've been thinking about the Christmas story. It seems that we usually emphasize most the cradle and the nativity. We like the scene of the baby nestling comfortably in a manger of straw, while all kinds of extremely well-behaved animals stand around patiently waiting for their photograph to be taken for Christmas cards. But there is a real danger that in concentrating on the crib, we may miss the ultimate significance of it.

We forget that the crib is quite meaningless apart from the cross of Calvary. In fact, we can only rightly understand the crib of Jesus' birth, as well as the rest of Jesus' life and ministry, in light of his crucifixion on the cross.

The crossless crib

There's something beautiful and delightful about the birth of the Christ child. In the cynical and rapidly aging world in which we live, we've become accustomed to seeing bloodshed, violence, hatred, and suffering. One of the wonderful things about the Christmas season is that for a few short hours we concentrate not on violence, but on something unbelievably innocent and beautiful—the baby in the crib. And the beauty of this baby's birth led to the wonder of the Savior's life.

However, if we concentrate only on the innocent baby's birth, which led to the sinless Savior's life, we arrive at a very unpleasant conclusion: The life Jesus lived ultimately condemns the life we live. When we evaluate our lives against that one life, we can only admit the hopelessness and helplessness of our condition. We cannot live as he lived, and we cannot undo the consequences of our own shortcomings.

If we only look at the crib, we arrive at a point of despair. For the beautiful crib led to Jesus' majestic and superb example, which leads us to a sense of helpless inadequacy. A crossless crib leads to hopelessness.

The Crownless Crib

If we read Scripture very carefully, we will recognize that before the crib there was the "crown" of Jesus. And after the crib, that crown will be replaced. In other words, the life, ministry, death, and resurrection of our Lord Jesus on earth served as a glorious interlude in the eternal reign of the Lord of all glory.

This baby that was born came from eternity. While he was on earth, he prayed, "Father, glorify me in your own presence with the glory that I had in your presence before the world existed" (John 17:5, NRSV). We cannot really consider the Son of God in the crib apart from the Son seated on the throne of heaven. We should always beware of the doctrine of the crownless crib. For if we forget the crown, we will lose our sense of who Jesus really is.

The cribless Cross

I suppose that Jesus could have just stepped off his heavenly throne for a moment, come to earth and died for us, and gone straight back to the throne again. He could have bypassed the crib and gone straight to the cross. But God, in Christ, chose to become one of us. The babe was born, went through childhood and adolescence, and grew into young adulthood, managing the same routines and crises as all humans do.

We must never downplay the humanity of our Savior, underscored by his birth in the crib. We can be confident that he understands us and our world. We can pray to him, knowing that he truly knows us and all our needs.

The Christian's crib, Cross, and Crown

The Lord Jesus explained that membership in God's kingdom involved being born from above. The apostle Peter tells us that we must be born anew, have a new seed in us, and become partakers of the divine nature. The apostle Paul writes that Christ must not only be born in our lives, but must grow and mature in them as well. Paul longed to see Christ fully formed in the lives of believers. In short, Christians need to

be clear that there is a crib in our lives—the miracle of regeneration. Just as the eternal Son of God was born in a stable, so the risen Christ is born in our lives.

I want you to ask yourself a question: *Has Jesus Christ been born in my life?* You say, how do you answer that question? Well, if I were to ask, "Have you been born?" you'd probably say, "Of course." And if I asked, "How do you know? Do you remember your birth?" your answer would probably be no. You would know you had been born simply because you're alive now. In the same way, if Christ has been born in you, his life will be reflected in your life. Not only will Christ be reflected in you, but that reflection will become clearer and clearer. There ought to be an increasing likeness to Jesus Christ in your ongoing experience.

A crib, in which the miracle of rebirth and regeneration takes place, is fundamental to our spiritual experience. But the crib isn't enough. If Christ has been born in us, we must grow and mature as his disciples. Jesus said, "If any want to become my followers, let them deny themselves and take up their cross daily and follow me" (Luke 9:23, NRSV).

What does it mean to take up our cross daily and follow him? Many people who talk of "bearing their cross" mean something like trying bravely to put up with what they can't alter. Sometimes they talk about a bad marriage, saying, "Well, that's my cross." Or they talk about an illness. Or they talk about their kids driving them up a wall. These things should never be confused with crosses. A cross is not a brave attempt to put up with what you can't change.

"Taking up our cross" means submitting our wills to God's will. Jesus willingly accepted God's will for our sake, and it cost him his life. Those who invite Jesus Christ into their lives must identify with the will of God as surely as Christ identified himself with the eternal purposes of the Father.

Our contemporary society has fallen ill to the disease of meaninglessness, a sickness that leads to hopelessness and superficiality. So many people have given in. "Life is falling apart," they say. "I'm just not going to think about it." So we live shallow, superficial lives. Yet just below the surface, a fear about the future eats away at us. We can't completely avoid the nagging issues of life.

Christians, however, need not remain in such a Slough of Despond. For believers there is not only a crib and a cross, but the sure promise of a crown. We will live through all eternity with the risen, ascended, King of kings and Lord of lords, who will wear a glorious crown. And we too will receive crowns for faithful service to him.

Now then, this produces a different breed of person in society. Instead of focusing on the material world—worrying about inflation or the nasty people we must deal with; trying desperately to preserve our youth because we're so frightened of aging; tightly gripping all that we own because that's all we've got—we can live confidently and with hope because we live in the light of the crown.

Those without a crib have yet to experience new life in Christ. Those without a cross have not given over their self-centered lives in exchange for the abundant God-centered life. And those without a crown have no depth or sense of hope. Crib, cross, and crown—are all three present in your life?

christmas now

Straw Your throne,
  cattle Your companions,
  creatures made by Thee.
Jesus—birthed a man child.
King's crown left on Heaven's seat,
Cared for by a child
  who hardly counts her age in double figures!
Poor, scared, not wanting to drop You,
  precious Baby King!

Hard the earth,
  no other place to lay Your kingly head.
No need to count the stars—
You know their number.
They clapped their hands when You
  created them.
Glad to shine then,
  glad to shine now,
  reminding You of home!

High Your cross where reigns death,
   strange seat to share with such a monarch.
How is it that You take Your place
   on such a bed of blood and pain?
For me, You say?
Straw Your throne?
Hard the earth?
High Your cross?
Cold Your grave?
For me?!

Cold the tomb of cruel reality!
Crying out in disbelief
   to find itself so used.
Oh, regal Savior,
   swathed in swaddling bands again
As in birth,
   so in death,
Royal robes of wrath!

Hot the hell that welcomed You.
Better far—the straw,
   the earth,
   the cross,
   the tomb—than this!

A broken heart of love lies shattered
   in this place.
A hideous smile of hate
   twists Satan's face.
Remind me that my baby King
   knew all of this
   before He came in embryonic form.

Oh, thank You little King,
My Christmas
My Delight
My Joy
My All!
My party will be tinged with tears of troubled thoughts,
As I gaze in Your manger bed;
Straw Your throne,
Hard the earth,
High Your cross,
Cold Your grave,
Hot Your hell!

Christmas now!
Great Your glory, Lord.
Reached Your Father down
Swaddling You in swathing bands of light;
You, who do delight His eyes—
Treasure of His heart!

Jesus, Jewel of heaven:
    fire Your throne,
    earth Your footstool now.
Empty cross and open tomb,
    a witness to the hell
You overcame—
    for Mighty King You are.

Straw Your throne,
Hard the earth,
High Your cross,
Cold Your grave,
Hot Your hell,
CHRISTMAS NOW!

epiphany

he word *epiphany* is defined as "a revelatory manifestation of a divine being." This dictionary definition accurately captures the biblical concept of epiphany. Simply stated, an epiphany is God appearing and revealing himself to human beings in some tangible way. Scripture points us toward two specific epiphanies.

> For the grace of God that brings salvation has appeared to all men. It teaches us to say "No" to ungodliness and worldly passions, and to live self-controlled, upright and godly lives in this present age, while we wait for the blessed hope—the glorious appearing of our great God and Savior, Jesus Christ, who gave himself for us to redeem us from all wickedness and to purify for himself a people that are his very own, eager to do what is good. (Titus 2:11-14)

We find the first epiphany in verse 11, "the grace of God that brings salvation has appeared to all men." The second is in verse 13, "we wait for the blessed hope—the glorious ap-

pearing of our great God and Savior, Jesus Christ." The first epiphany has already taken place; the second is yet to come. In the life and ministry of Jesus Christ, God manifested himself on earth in humility and suffering. He will come again, only this time in glory and triumph.

So, at this moment in human history, we live suspended between two epiphanies. What a privilege! And what a responsibility! We must live in the light of both divine appearances.

At Christmas time we think automatically of the first appearing. Titus 2:11 is one of the most succinct statements of the Christmas story you'll ever find. At Christmas, God appeared in the flesh to bring salvation. This appearance has taught us certain things: "to say 'No' to ungodliness and worldly passions, and to live self-controlled, upright and godly lives in this present age, while we wait for the blessed hope—the glorious appearing of our great God and Savior, Jesus Christ."

The first appearing gives us the knowledge and hope to live differently now. We might call this first appearing the *gracious epiphany,* because God appeared in grace. We might call the second appearing the *glorious epiphany,* because we look forward to the glory of Christ's second coming.

The initial epiphany was not only an unbelievable demonstration of grace, but also the means of our salvation. In the most important realms of life, men and women cannot pull themselves up by their own bootstraps. That's the last thing self-sufficient people want to hear, but it's the one thing they need to hear. We cannot save ourselves from the past or the unknown but inevitable consequences of the future. We cannot make ourselves fit for heaven *without this initial appearing of God in our midst.* Christ was the ambassador from heaven, holding within himself the means of getting us there.

How shall we then live, in light of this first appearing?

With gratefulness for our salvation, with a real desire to live holy lives, with a new ability to say no to the things that drag us away from God's will for our lives.

How shall we then live, in light of the appearing yet to come? With greater passion to live holy lives in anticipation of his coming. We must give an account for the salvation purchased for us at such a great price to heaven. We will live with hope and joy, confident that the God-man, whose first appearance radically transformed the very fabric of our lives, is coming again in power and glory.

> At that time the sign of the Son of Man will appear in the sky, and all the nations of the earth will mourn. They will see the Son of Man coming on the clouds of the sky, with power and great glory. And he will send his angels with a loud trumpet call, and they will gather his elect from the four winds, from one end of the heavens to the other. (Matt. 24:30-31)

The babe who came to us in a lowly country manger, in the quiet contemplation of a young girl's life, will appear to us again in awesome glory, recognized around the world. This, indeed, is the glorious epiphany.

> Do not let your hearts be troubled. Trust in God; trust also in me. In my Father's house are many rooms; if it were not so, I would have told you. I am going there to prepare a place for you. And if I go and prepare a place for you, I will come back and take you to be with me that you also may be where I am. (John 14:1-3)

For now, we travel to Bethlehem, one by one, to see God for ourselves. Someday, God will gather up each one of his children, and we will return with him in all glory and praise.

A Time For Giving

What are you giving for Christmas?

God the Father scattered the Milky Way across the skies, hung Saturn's rings in place, and thought about Christmas. God the Son, working in unity with the Father, fashioned the lumbering oxen and the gentle cow with his creative power, and thought often of the day when the Father would speak the Word, and he would become flesh. On that day he would gaze with "baby eyes" upon the very creatures he had made. God the Holy Spirit, moving as a shadow upon the face of the waters in Genesis days, knew one day it would be necessary to move again. This time he would overshadow Mary's womb, that "the Holy thing" to be born of her should be called the "Son of God."

Adam, walking with God in the Garden of Eden, oblivious to such names as Bethlehem, Herod, Egypt, Gethsemane, and Calvary, chose in one appalling moment the company of Satan rather than God. Adam opted for the kingship of self rather than the kingdom of God, and the bondage of sin rather than the glorious liberty of God's children. But even at that time Adam heard the Maker's promise: The promised Seed

would bruise the serpent's head. God was saying, "Christmas is coming, Adam." And I believe that, even there in the Garden, the Holy Trinity—Father, Son, and Holy Spirit—celebrated the Christmas redemption that would come someday.

Many of God's people throughout time thought about God's special gift, and offered their own gifts in thankful response. These gifts are not boxes decorated with tinsel, silver bells, and Father Christmases, but unique contributions to the tremendous story of God's special gift. In quiet sadness Jeremiah contemplated the massacre of the infants. Hosea joyfully thanked God for the escape to Egypt. Micah let the world know where Jesus would be born. And Isaiah told us that God's gift would come special delivery, a son born of a virgin. This son would be called Wonderful Counselor, Mighty God, Everlasting Father, Prince of Peace.

Four hundred years later, as an elderly Elizabeth was thinking about those promised gifts, God was busy wrapping his Christmas present from heaven in human flesh. Christmas came early for Elizabeth. When Elizabeth welcomed her cousin Mary, the outcast, ostracized, pregnant young girl, God pulled back the wrapping paper just a little, to let her have a peek at his present. Elizabeth's own baby leaped in her womb for joy, and she was filled with the Holy Spirit, and said: "Blessed are you among women, and blessed is the child you will bear! But why am I so favored, that the mother of my Lord should come to me? As soon as the sound of your greeting reached my ears, the baby in my womb leaped for joy" (Luke 1:42-45).

Encouraged and strengthened by her cousin, Mary also prepared. She believed the anointed One must come and soon, and by her holy character made ready to acknowledge her Messiah and yield her allegiance to him. God couldn't have a Christmas without a Mary. He needed more than just a devout person, someone who attended synagogue and said her prayers. The child Christ needed a body to live in!

When God became a baby, he knew he'd to compress,
His vastness, glory, all that power, into littleness.
A baby was the answer, but where to find the one,
The one who'd say, "Be born in me—
Oh, let me bear your Son"?

Would Mary be the earthly vehicle for God's divine action?
"Now wait a minute," the devil must have whispered to Mary.
"You've got everything going for you—

You're engaged to be married, what will people say,
When you say that your baby is conceived a new
way?
Just imagine their startled incredulity,
When you say so sincerely, "God gave it to me!"

But Mary offered the gift of her body. She whispered, "Behold the handmaid of the Lord; be it unto me according to thy word" (Luke 1:38, KJV).

Christmas is a time for giving. The prophets gave their promises. Elizabeth gave her praise. Mary gave her body. Joseph gave his reputation. The innkeeper gave his stable, the shepherds, their time. And God gave his Son. Tell me, do you see *your* present there?

What are you giving for Christmas?

choosing to be chosen

'm sure God had chosen Mary to bear Jesus, yet he allows us to choose to be chosen! It is one thing to give God our Sunday attention or five minutes of devotional time, but another matter entirely to yield our bodies—our whole lives—to do his will. Yet we live within our bodies and cannot serve him without them. Didn't the apostle Paul remind us of this when he wrote, "I appeal to you therefore, brothers and sisters, by the mercies of God, to present your bodies as a living sacrifice, holy and acceptable to God, which is your spiritual worship" (Rom. 12:1, NRSV).

Presenting our bodies to God is part of our spiritual worship. My husband defines a body as "an earthly vehicle whereby a spiritual entity gets around in a physical environment." God dignified the human body through creation, the incarnation, and in redemption. Mary teaches us that we need to yield all of ourselves—body, mind, and spirit—to him.

How many Marys, Lord, were there?
How many times did you try?
How often did Gabriel venture

Through the myriad stars of the sky?
How many minuscule humans?
How many a devout little maid
Heard your request for a body
And answered you thus so afraid?
"My love, Lord, you have it.
My will, Lord, 'tis thine.
I, to mighty Jehovah, my worship assign,
But my body, my body, my body 'tis mine!"

How many Marys, Lord, were there,
Till Gabriel found her at prayer?
How many angels in glory
Were wondrously envious of her?
And how did it feel, Lord, to see her,
And watch at your feet as she fell,
As she yielded her soul and her spirit
And gave you a body as well?

"My love, Lord, you have it.
My will, Lord, 'tis thine.
I, to mighty Jehovah, my worship assign.
And my body, my body, my body 'tis Thine!"

RESPONDING TO THE CHRIST CHILD

Glory to God in the highest, and on earth peace, good will toward men.
(Luke 2:14, KJV)

Years ago, a friend of mine in England heard that there was going to be a peace rally in Liverpool. Liverpool is a port city with lots of dock workers, many of whom were "pink" or "red" in their politics. These "dockers" were organizing the peace rally, inviting anybody who wanted to say something on the subject of peace. My preacher friend decided to go as a minister of the gospel.

He got up among all the communists and began to preach about the gospel of peace. He told them that peace was not going to come about through political manipulation. Peace would come only when people were liberated from the wickedness in their own hearts, when they were so free within that they stopped automatically responding from sinful, selfish motivation.

The crowd, of course, wasn't too enthusiastic about my friend's preaching. His message flew in the face of their proposed political strategies and solutions. But fortunately, something happened that helped my friend's cause considerably.

The organizers had dressed a lot of little boys in white robes with little wings on their backs and given them poles

with papier mâché peace doves mounted on top. These little angels carrying their peace doves had marched in front during the rally's procession. While my friend was preaching, all of a sudden one of the little angels clobbered another little angel over the head with his peace dove. A fight broke out.

"I assure you I didn't rig the fight," my friend said later. "But what a great illustration of just how far sentimental talk will lead us towards peace on earth and good will to all. Such talk is utter nonsense until we know the reality of liberation from our iniquity. And unless we know this liberation, we might as well stop talking about peace on earth for people of good will, because people of goodwill don't exist if they are not released from their sin."

> He came to that which was his own, but his own did not receive him. Yet to all who received him, to those who believed in his name, he gave the right to become children of God—children born not of natural descent, nor of human decision, . . . but born of God. (John 1:11-13)

We have been to the manger. We have met God there. We have begun to understand what it means that he came to visit us. The man Jesus said, and continues to say, "Open your life to me. Allow me to come in and bring light into your darkness, life to your deadness, and truth to your confusion. Repent of your old way of life. Commit yourself, your life, your future, to me." The coming of that Christ child ultimately means that we have a decision to make.

And while we talk sentimentally about peace on earth and goodwill toward all, the Bible tells us that peace and goodwill can happen only from the inside out. The Christ child must be born within each one of us. And only the

Holy Spirit can release us from the power of our sin, self-delusion, and lostness. Only as his light dawns within us and begins to transform every aspect of our lives can we become all that we were meant to be.

A CHRISTMAS PRAYER

eavenly Father,

Thank you for Christmas time and for the Christ child in the manger. But the birth of your Son is interwoven with his spotless life, death, and resurrection. We stand as sinners in the face of such perfection, love, and grace.

Now, dear Lord, we bow quietly before you, thankful that, through your Son, you revealed to us the truth about ourselves. Teach us what it means to allow your peace to reign in our lives. And may the fullness of the real meaning of Christmas transform us into the people you have designed us to be. Amen.